STAYING FAITHFUL TODAY

When this book first appeared in 1981, the crisis of fidelity in our culture and
the church had already begun. Thousands of priests and religious
women and men had abandoned their vows, and marriages and families
were in crisis. Through it all, I wondered *why?* I concluded that our
church and culture had not reached the tipping point in which they
were able to realize the breakdown of fidelity to God, self, friendships,
country, marriage, and celibacy. Of course, we were just singing in the
rain or, more ominously, whistling in the dark. Our capacity for denial
and delusion regarding our most precious values was—and is still
today—unnerving.

Since then, our church has suffered the priest sex abuse tragedy and
a scandalous failure to be celibate. And the church's people have lost
respect for authority, adopted a reckless disregard for the sanctity of
marriage, and become addicted to the latest fads, including but not lim-
ited to drugs and alcohol. I believe the crisis of fidelity has now reached
dangerous levels both for the church and its people, and I am convinced
that the point I made in the first edition of *Staying Faithful* is now more
relevant than ever. That is why I have titled this edition *Staying Faithful
Today*.

Facing the loss of fidelity to the basic principles of life, major religious
leaders have developed the "Manhattan Declaration: A Call of Christian
Conscience." In announcing this call, Archbishop Timothy Dolan said
that the deepest vocation crisis is marital fidelity and that if successful

and holy unions of marriage and the family had flourished, there would be many more seminarians and priests than we have today. The Manhattan Declaration summarizes its goals and purpose on its website as follows:

> Because the sanctity of human life, the dignity of marriage as a union of husband and wife, and the freedom of conscience and religion are foundational principles of justice and the common good, we are compelled by our Christian faith to speak and act in their defense. In this declaration we affirm: 1) the profound, inherent, and equal dignity of every human being as a creature fashioned in the very image of God, possessing inherent rights of equal dignity and life; 2) marriage as a conjugal union of man and woman, ordained by God from the creation, and historically understood by believers and non-believers alike, to be the most basic institution in society and; 3) religious liberty, which is grounded in the character of God, the example of Christ, and the inherent freedom and dignity of human beings created in the divine image.[1]

I like both the content of this declaration and the strong language in which it is written. It is unambiguous, clear, forceful, and visionary. For too long we have appeared weak regarding the issues here. It's not that we didn't keep the issues on the books, but our public commitment seemed shrouded in the fear of speaking up and being prophetic in public discourse. Our peculiar silence in recent decades is now resulting in the potential ruin of our most cherished values and institutions.

Some prominent columnists are addressing this very issue. *New York Times* writer David Brooks, in his column "The Broken Society" in March 2010, quotes prominent British writer Philip Blond:

> Over the past generation we have witnessed two revolutions, both of which liberated the individual and decimated local associations. First, there was a revolution from the left: a

cultural revolution that displaced traditional manners and mores; a legal revolution that emphasized individual rights instead of responsibilities; and a welfare revolution in which social workers displaced mutual aid societies and self-organized associations.[2]

The sixth commandment says, "You shall not commit adultery." Stated positively, the commandment means, "You shall practice fidelity in your marriages." The high-profile adulteries among our political leaders, sports figures, and media celebrities contain a consistent picture of the stalwart wife trying to appear courageous by the side of her unfaithful spouse. I see them carrying the shame, pain, and hurt of the dream of marital love shattered. To think that a certain prominent presidential candidate betrayed his wife and continued to lie about it while she was suffering cancer stuns the conscience and arouses anger. To watch a United States governor admit, while holding the hand of his pained wife at a press conference, that he paid thousands of dollars for a few hours with a prostitute confounds both reason and common sense. It is clear evidence of the careless dismissal of marriage and the promises to be faithful in sickness and in health until death.

This case was barely through the news cycle when another prominent leader in our government traveled thousands of miles to South America to break his marital bond. Not only did his wife mourn with remembrances of their early love and the sacrifices she made for his career, but moreover, she mourned for her four children, who were left confused, embarrassed, and brokenhearted as well.

Infidelities—among the rich and poor, the famous and the infamous, the government class and the Hollywood celebrities and the everyday middle-class families—are painfully well known. Finally, and even more tragic, are the infidelities of priest sex-abusers whose sins have affected the faith of thousands of Catholics, the lives of the victims, and the credibility of the church.

Even when a moderate commentator raises the idea that Christianity would be good for the public sinners, the culture arises to shut the mouth of such a dissenter. Questioning this strange reaction, *New York Times* columnist Ross Douthat lamented the notion that the public square is no place to champion religion. In his column, "Let's Talk About Faith," he defended Fox News commentator Brit Hume's right to give advice to embattled champion golfer Tiger Woods, who was facing a marital scandal. Douthat quotes Hume, who suggested that Woods should consider converting to Christianity, saying that, "He's said to be a Buddhist. I don't think that faith offers the kind of forgiveness and redemption that is offered by the Christian faith." Douthat claimed that a number of people declared that this comment was the most outrageous thing they ever heard, and he went on to say, "Hume's words were replayed by Jon Stewart on the *Daily Show*, to shocked laughter from the audience. They were denounced across the blogosphere as evidence of chauvinism, bigotry and gross stupidity. MSNBC's Keith Olbermann claimed, absurdly, that Hume had tried to 'threaten Tiger Woods into becoming a Christian.'" Without agreeing with what Hume said, Douthat argued simply that, "The idea that religion is too mysterious, too complicated or too personal to be debated on cable television just ensures that it will never be debated at all."[3]

While Douthat was simply supporting Hume's right to discuss religion (and the inherent differences among various beliefs) on television, I would add that open conversation about it in the public square is an *essential* way to get the message out to the culture. I would also go so far as to agree with Hume. *Why shouldn't we help people be converted to Christ?* St. Peter's first sermon was a call to conversion. Without conversions there would never have been a church. Without conversions today, we would lose the dynamism converts bring to us. St. Paul was a powerful, persistent preacher of Christ and incredibly blessed by his evangelizing mission. And thank God for the TV ads, "Catholics Come Home," which invite inactive Catholics to come back to our faith.

In his book, *Souls in Transition: The Religious and Spiritual Lives of Emerging Adults*, Notre Dame sociologist Christian Smith explores what *Wall Street Journal* columnist Naomi Schaefer Riley, in her article "The Fate of the Spirit," calls the "wobbly religious lives of young people emerging into adulthood." It's not a pretty picture and should be an emergency call to our church, other faith communities, and all people of goodwill to link faith and fidelity through teaching, discipline, and visible witness. In Riley's column she wonders, "So why are most emerging adults so morally unmoored and religiously alienated?" She writes:

> Mr. Smith suggests that religious institutions haven't done a very good job at educating kids in even the most basic tenets of their faiths. And religious parents often shirk their duties, too, perhaps believing the "cultural myth" that they have no influence over their children once they hit puberty. Mr. Smith has found, to the contrary, that, when it comes to religious faith and practice, "who and what parents were and are" is more likely to "stick" with emerging adults than the beliefs and habits of their teenage friends.[4]

I believe these contemporary markers are signs of discontent with infidelity, and they criticize not just the culture but also the timidity of the churches. Fidelity is intrinsically related to faith. I think often of St. Anselm's powerful mantra, "Believe that you may understand," meaning that you must take a stand in order to understand. Faith in God is critical for all the other fidelities that I examine in this book. The extensive literature of covenant in the Bible is "Exhibit A" for God's fidelity to us. Our belief in God is the basis of staying faithful.

OUR FIDELITY JOURNEY AHEAD

In *Staying Faithful Today*, I join you in the quest for fidelity. We all begin with the best of intentions to be faithful. This is why we love weddings, baptisms, new beginnings in all walks of life. The innocence attracts us and gives us hope. The relationships captivate us. The implicit magic of love gives us the courage to think we will keep our promises. A deep look at such good starts reminds us of the old proverb, "Well begun is half done."

I will walk with you through the winding paths of today's culture, which is ambiguous about God. In our best moments we know intuitively that stable relationships require a conviction that God exists, but even more important is the knowledge that God is a living being who thinks a lot of us. Faith in a living and loving God does not begin with us. It begins with God's lavish interest in giving us the gift of faith that is the ground of fidelity. God always practices what he preaches.

I believe you and I both hear the ancient questions, "Who am I? Where did I come from? Where am I going?" Modernity's fast pace tries to sidetrack us from the silence and time needed for the "well-examined life." Shakespeare advised us to be true to our own selves and, then it will follow, as the sun the day, we will not be false to anyone. Healthy solitude and honest self-evaluation generate fidelity to self, which is a condition of being faithful to others.

Like you, I cherish the friends who have come into my life. I wonder if I have nurtured these gifts. We know that old friends are the best friends, the miracle of a sustained relationship amid the interruptions of life. The durability of friendship can only exist if we pay attention to it. One of life's most enjoyable pleasures cannot be accessible unless we treasure the good people who have enriched our lives. Very few of us live like hermits. We are fundamentally tribal, although now we call it belonging to communities. We were made to live in community, be that our family, our church, our country, or the clubs that attract us. To thrive in the various communities, we must exercise the responsibilities of membership. If that sounds too legalistic, think of it as using the vast range of our glorious freedom to enhance communities with our time, talent, and treasure.

While I am not married, I greatly admire and fully support the millions of couples who struggle to make marriage work. I have found that faithful couples have strengthened my commitment to the priesthood. And I pray that God's gift of fidelity makes me of use to those worried about their relationships. Marriage promises are the most frequently made and profound in our culture. Couples benefit from faith, prayer, divine help, and the support of all who weep at weddings, smile at babies, and look with pride on couples who have learned and lived the time-honored secrets of success in marriage.

Finally, I share with you a few thoughts on the priesthood. I thank God for the spirit of hope and renewal he has given me and a host of priests I have been privileged to know. I have been depressed and discouraged by the scandals and public disdain of recent years. But at the same time, God has given me a circle of faithful priests and lay friends who have been rays of light and love and hope. The fundamentals of fidelity are brief and simple, even if they might be tough to practice. What else are love, friendship, self understanding, God's graces, the pleasures of patriotism and Mother Church about, if not forms of fidelity that make up the whole person?

I will use stories, studies, advice that comes from others' experiences, examples from popular and classical culture, and other forms of practical use, much as I did at the opening of this introduction to show all forms of fidelity. I think this book will work best with small groups, book clubs, couples' groups, and parish staff training. To this end, I present starter ideas at the conclusion of each chapter.

With prayer for continuous help from the Holy Spirit, let us begin this journey.

CHAPTER ONE

IF YOU DON'T LOVE, YOU WILL NOT BE FAITHFUL

"Love lifted me. Love lifted me.
When I was down and out, Love lifted me."
Gospel Song

WHAT DOES IT MEAN TO STAY FAITHFUL?
Fidelity is the practical expression of love. Fidelity is a love that is supported by loyalty and courage. Fidelity is keeping your promises to God, family, and country. It is having the courage to mean what you say and say what you mean. Fidelity requires courage to make and keep your promises—the kind of courage that provides you with the creativity and imagination with which to find unique ways to be faithful. Fidelity is staying true to your wedding promises, spoken in the presence of your faith community. It is living the vows you made as a priest or religious in the presence of a bishop at your ordination or before a religious superior, witnessed by the members of the order or congregation.

Fidelity is what our presidents need when they take the oath of office on Inauguration Day. It is what new candidates to the Supreme Court and judges at every level of society need when they promise to uphold the U.S. Constitution and the law of the land. It is what is expected of anyone who signs a contract. Fidelity is the common coinage for a society built on trust and character. We expect people in authority to keep

1

their word and be responsible in their behavior. Fidelity is the soul of what is often called the "social contract."

Starry-eyed young couples put great emotion into their marital promises, but they may not realize the challenges that lie ahead to keeping those promises. They will need the grace of God and the support of their families, friends, and the culture itself to keep them. They will need faith, prayer, and wisdom to withstand all the vagaries of human relationships—from the first quarrels, to the little betrayals, to the rough patches life always presents. Couples should read that beautiful old form of the *Exhortation Before Marriage* again and again, at the beginning of every month. Here is one powerful quote from that lovely text:

> Because these words (of your wedding vows) involve such solemn obligations, it is most fitting that you rest the security of your wedded life upon the great principle of self-sacrifice. And so today you begin your married life by the voluntary and complete surrender of your individual lives in the interest of that deeper and wider life you are to have in common.... There will be problems which might be difficult, but genuine love can make them easy and perfect love can make them a joy.[1]

The same is true of the fresh-faced new priest hearing himself called "Father" and even of the older, second-career candidate who brings the experience of the university of hard knocks to his new ministry. The Catholic parish is an interesting boot camp for the newly ordained. The honeymoon is brief and the sacrificial altar is almost eternal. Parishioners expect the priest to be a believer, to be working on his spiritual growth, to be a real human being, and to give evidence that he is a man of prayer. Fidelity applies to the people as well as to the priest. It is a persistent quest for holiness. Fr. Cipriano, a Mexican priest in the early part of the last century, knew how to say this in everyday language. Archbishop Joseph Gomez, in *Men of Brave Heart,* quotes Cipriano, saying:

To be a saint is to have the intention of doing all things for God. How rich and easy is the spiritual life! Why do you eat? To have the strength to serve God. Why do you sleep? Why do you obey? Not because your superior has a book in his hand, but to serve God.... If all that you do, you do for God, how can you do anything evil? Avoid wondering if what you do is the will of God, and make sure your intention is right and pure.[2]

The diocesan candidate for ordination makes promises of fidelity to his bishop, who first asks him, "Do you promise respect and obedience to me and my successors?" Normally in a packed church, in the presence of his family and friends and a large representation of priests, the candidate replies, "I do." In his homily, the bishop lays out the expectations of a priest, telling the candidate, "You must apply your energies to the duty of teaching in the name of Christ, the chief Teacher. Share with all mankind the word of God you have received with joy. Meditate on the law of God, believe what you read, teach what you believe, practice what you teach."[3] The church wisely has the whole congregation sing the Litany of Saints over him as he prostrates himself on the floor before the altar. He will need all the graces he can get.

What Does Scripture Say About Fidelity?

The Bible has a number of ways of speaking about fidelity, especially God's faithfulness to us, but also our promises to him. The Bible tells the story of a God who makes promises to us and never fails to fulfill them. The psalms often look at God's fidelity to Israel. This is especially true in his promises to King David that his posterity will never disappear. Psalm 89 clearly spells this out. God speaks:

> I will establish his line forever,
>   and his throne as long as the heavens endure.
> If his children forsake my law
>   and do not walk according to my ordinances,
> if they violate my statutes

and do not keep my commandments,
then I will punish their transgression with the rod
and their iniquity with scourges;
but I will not remove from him my steadfast love,
or be false to my faithfulness.
I will not violate my covenant,
or alter the word that went forth from my lips.
Once and for all I have sworn by my holiness;
I will not lie to David.
His line shall continue forever,
and his throne endure before me like the sun.
It shall be established forever like the moon,
an enduring witness in the skies. (Psalm 89:29–37)

God's fidelity to David and his descendants is only truly fulfilled in Jesus, son of David and son of God. In his message to Mary at the Annunciation, the angel Gabriel tells her that her child "will be great, and will be called Son of the Most High, and the Lord God will give to him the throne of his ancestor David" (Luke 1:32).

Signs of God's fidelity to us appear all over Scripture. In the story of the Fall, God hints of future redemption in his words to the evil one,

I will put enmity between you and the woman,
and between your offspring and hers;
he will strike your head,
and you will strike his heel. (Genesis 3:15)

God sets a rainbow in the sky to assure Noah of the permanence of his covenantal promises. God promises Abraham a land and a people, which eventually happens. God comes in a burning bush to Moses both to reveal in more detail his identity as Yahweh and to promise to liberate his people from slavery, an event that occurs in the crossing of the Red Sea and is maintained during the people's lengthy pilgrimage in the desert. God sends prophets to the kings to urge them to recognize his

4

promises and have faith in them. Even in exile, God assures his people through the prophet Ezekiel of a future return their homeland.

Read all of Psalm 136, which is a hymn that celebrates the history of God's fidelity expressed in his loving mercy. The psalm is like a Catholic litany, with each of its twenty-six verses ending with the refrain, "for his steadfast love endures forever." In meditating on the Last Supper narrative that says Jesus sang a song before going to his death, I have imagined that he chanted Psalm 136, which perfectly summarizes God's fidelity. It is clear that only in Christ does God's fidelity to his promises become absolutely true, as noted by the author of the letter to the Hebrews:

> Now faith is the assurance of things hoped for, the conviction of things not seen. Indeed, by faith our ancestors received approval. By faith we understand that the worlds were prepared by the word of God, so that what is seen was made from things that are not visible. (Hebrews 11:1–3)

Jesus is the very perfection of fidelity. He said he came to do the Father's will, and he did it. In spite of the slowness of people to understand him, the betrayals he was to experience, the foolishness of apostles who argued about power, the cruel words spoken to him on the cross, Jesus journeyed on to be faithful to the end.

During Holy Week, through one of my devotional customs, I arouse my feeling for the Passion of Christ by listening to the choir and orchestra performing the music of Theodore Dubois's "The Seven Last Words of Jesus." His evocation of the first Word of Jesus from the cross never fails to move me. The priests scream, "He is guilty, take him, Let us crucify him!" The people yell, "Be his blood on us then, and on our children!" The soldiers do the mob's bidding and nail Jesus to the wood. Dubois surrounds these words with harsh, dissonant music, pounding drums, and a sense of evil chaos. I think of Jesus with his arms uplifted on the wood in the posture of prayer. In the very moment of his saving the world, the cross is his altar. With his outstretched arms raised in the prayer position, he gazes on his noisy creatures, who are shouting with blood lust, yelling with scorn. Ever since his birth at Bethlehem, he was destined for this hour. His long journey was ending. Although weakened by beatings, punches, spitting, and nails, he will not let ingratitude deter him. While it is hard for me to watch Mel Gibson's *The Passion of the Christ*, I know that his visual of Jesus bound to the cross are even more accurate than his grating scourging at the pillar. Let me say this, without any exaggeration: The Passion is the Son of God's unsurpassed evidence of what fidelity—with its courage, splendid love, and perseverance—ultimately means. The crucified Jesus is absolute icon of what "staying faithful" really means.

With a stroke of musical genius, Dubois gives Christ's reply the extraordinary peaceful, melodic, and healing blessing from the cross when he sings, "Father, forgive them, for they know not what they do." It's the only way to *stay faithful* by pouring coals of fire on the consuming sinfulness of the mob at Calvary. At that moment Jesus could truthfully say to himself and to us, "And I, when I am lifted up from the earth, will draw all people to myself" (John 12:32). Then, as the moment of his death arrived, he remained faithful to the end and said, "It is finished" (John 19:30). He showed us the cost of fidelity. It is one of the most difficult virtues, which may account for the enormous resistance many people have in living its demands.

Thirty years ago, Benedict XVI, as Joseph Ratzinger, wrote his most influential book, *Introduction to Christianity*. In dealing with the mystery of the cross, he referred several times to the symbolism of Christ's outstretched arms, noting the interpretation given this by Fathers of the church:

> This is how the Church Fathers interpreted the arms of the Lord outstretched on the Cross. They saw in them, first of all, the primordial form of the Christian position of prayer, the attitude of the *orantes* so movingly portrayed in the pictures in the

catacombs. The arms of the crucified Christ thus show him to be the worshiper, a dimension that forms the specifically Christian element in the glorification of God. These open arms are also the expression of worship precisely because they express complete devotion to men, because they are a gesture of embrace, of full and undivided brotherliness.[4]

It is not only in his death that Jesus demonstrates his fidelity but also in his Resurrection. He promised to conquer death, and on Easter Sunday that's just what he did. Jesus was able to feel the loss of people caught in the process of dying. Thousands of people die every hour, even as thousands more are born. But whether we think of the infant or the centenarian, we affirm that we all bear within us the fear that we will be wiped out. Against the biological reality of death and the dissolution of the body is the seed of eternity that rebels against death. Within every human is the mystery of yet a new life given us by Christ. Believers every Sunday sing with joy the words of the Nicene Creed: "We look for the resurrection of the dead and the life of the world to come."

I was once driving with my friend Joe Lopez, the father of five grown children, to a ski slope in New Mexico. Joe liked to philosophize during our trips. He asked me, "What did Christ promise about what will happen after death?" I happened to have my Liturgy of the Hours with me, and I turned to a passage from Corinthians and read it to Joe. It was Paul's magnificent tribute to the truth about Christ's Resurrection and ours: "For the trumpet will sound, and the dead will be raised imperishable, and we will be changed. For this perishable body must put on imperishability, and this mortal body must put on immortality" (1 Corinthians 15:52b–53). It climaxes with the words that Handel's *Messiah* dramatically illustrates—our final resurrection from the dead. (I recommend you read all of 1 Corinthians 15.)

Several years ago, I wrote about this moment in my book, *The Seven Last Words of Jesus:*

7

In his seventh word, Jesus calmly and lovingly gave his life to God. . . . [Jesus] sensed as thoroughly as any human ever will the seed of eternity; he gathered his whole being in expectation of life after life. In the poet Dylan Thomas's imagery about dying, Jesus "raged against the dying of the light" in the sense that he rebelled against death as the end of everything. But then he went "gentle into that good night" because beyond it is the warmth of love beyond all telling and the light that will never be extinguished. The peacefulness of his seventh word is the biblical *shalom*, the perfect reconciliation with God that is the model and cause of such peace for every human being.[5]

WHAT DOES THE CHURCH SAY ABOUT FIDELITY?
The church always turns to the Word of God in Scripture when she wants to talk about fidelity. The church believes, with St. Paul, that she is the Body of Christ, the temple of the Holy Spirit, the very people of God. These three images contain the beliefs that have corresponding responsibilities. It is natural for the church to bond faith to fidelity and beliefs to commitments. For the church, the Nicene and Apostles Creeds are far more than statements to be believed; they are promises and vows that will shape our consciences, mold our attitudes, and sustain our actions. The creeds are miniature catechisms that tell us about our love relationship with God, who God is, what he has done, and what is our ultimate destiny.

If you want to know in detail the church's story of fidelity, study the *Catechism of the Catholic Church*. Its four pillars of creed, liturgy, morality, and prayer are firm foundations for your commitment to Christ, his Father, and the Holy Spirit. For a text that is perhaps more immediately accessible, I also recommend studying the Catholic bishops' adaptation of that catechism to the American scene under the title, *United States Catholic Catechism for Adults*. Every chapter begins with the story of a saint or some other outstanding American Catholic noted for his or her fidelity to Christ and to the spiritual and moral principles that are a sure guide to personal fulfillment and a loving, compassionate service to others, especially the poor.

In everyday life the church invites your fidelity to Christ's teachings in the beatitudes and his Sermon on the Mount (Matthew, 5—7), as well as the Ten Commandments and the practicing of the seven life-changing virtues: faith, hope, love, prudence, justice, disciplined self-restraint, and courage. The church encourages you to participate in regular Sunday worship where, in unity with God's people, your heart is nourished with God's Word and your whole being is made holy by taking Holy Communion.

At every Mass, the church puts on our lips the seven petitions of the Our Father. Every petition is a call to holiness. Jesus has given us the perfect fidelity prayer that transforms our souls by yearning that:

- God's holy name sanctify us.
- God's kingdom of love, justice, mercy and salvation penetrate our very bones.
- God's will become our will.
- We seek and enjoy our daily bread of food, clothing, and shelter but also seek the divine nutrition of Holy Eucharist.
- We forgive in order to be forgiven.
- We implore the Lord not to test us beyond our ability to carry the burden.
- We beg Jesus to give the graces of redemption from all our evil.

The Our Father is like a classic Renaissance painting that crowds the canvas with spiritual milk for beginners and meat for the mature.

After two thousand years, the church has inherited a number of rules and laws to help us stay faithful to Christ—rules for stable and permanent marriages, rules for lifetime priests, rules for public prayer. I believe that such rules work best for us when seen against the vision, principles, and relationship insights I offer in this chapter. The rules are marching orders, the vision and grace of God is food for the soul and for the journey. Empty souls, like empty stomachs, need nourishment. Lord, give us this day our daily bread.

IDEAS HAVE CONSEQUENCES AND OTHER THOUGHTS
by G.K. Chesterton

What does our basic code of conduct say? My first thought is to review accepted nuggets of modern wisdom such as: *Wake up early. Plan, but not too much. Take one day off per week. Read one book a week. Think positively.* These help when our house is in order, when our inner self is straightened out. But if our thoughts are crooked, how can we make them straight? If our heads are on backward, how can we move forward? I prefer the "ideas have consequences" approach, such as the remarkable writer G.K. Chesterton passed on to us. Here are a few creative thoughts from his most famous book, *Orthodoxy*:

"The modern world is full of old Christian virtues gone mad. The virtues have gone mad because they have been isolated from each other and are wandering alone. Thus some scientists care for truth; and their truth is pitiless. Thus some humanitarians only care for pity; and their pity (I am sorry to say) is often untruthful." [6]

"When you choose anything, you reject everything else." [7]

"Some dogma, we are told, was credible in the twelfth century, but it is not credible in the twentieth. You might as well say that a certain philosophy can be believed on Mondays, but cannot be believed on Tuesdays." [8]

CONCLUSION

In this chapter I have approached the meaning of fidelity from differing viewpoints. I wrote that fidelity is the practical expression of love. Fidelity is a love that is supported by loyalty and courage. Fidelity is keeping your promises to God, family, and flag. It is having the courage to mean what you say and say what you mean. It requires courage to make such a promise and perseverance to keep it. I applied this to the fidelity needed by newlyweds and young priests beginning their ministry.

I then explored the treatment of fidelity in Scripture, especially the way in which God kept his promises throughout salvation history. Then I showed how fidelity reaches its fulfillment in Christ, particularly in his passion, death, and resurrection. Fidelity at its summit is a love that lays down its life for the beloved. Finally, I reviewed the church's vision of fidelity as being the Body of Christ, the temple of the Spirit, and the people of God. The church explores fidelity in Scripture, explains it in the catechisms, and experiences it in liturgy and the moral and spiritual life of the members.

FOR PERSONAL APPLICATION

1. How have I advanced fidelity in my marriage or in other relationships?
2. How faithful have I been to prayer and Mass?
3. How am I passing on faith and fidelity to the children in my life?

FOR GROUP DISCUSSION

1. Ask each participant: What is your idea of fidelity?
2. Invite participants to tell stories of fidelity and infidelity.
3. How does our culture assist or undermine fidelity?
4. What are effective ways to stay faithful?

SCRIPTURE MEDITATION

I have said these things to you so that my joy may be in you, and that your joy may be complete.

This is my commandment, that you love one another as I have loved you. No one has greater love than this, to lay down one's life for one's friends. You are my friends if you do what I command you. I do not call you servants any longer, because the servant does not know what the master is doing; but I have called you friends, because I have made known to you everything that I have heard from my Father. You did not choose me but I chose you. And I appointed you to go and bear fruit, fruit that will last, so that the Father will give you whatever you ask him in my name. I am giving you these commands so that you may love one another. (John 15:11–17)

PROMISES

I pledge to be faithful to God by:

_____

_____

_____

_____

_____

_____

_____

_____

_____

_____

_____

_____

CHAPTER TWO

God Is Always Faithful to Us

On that day I will answer, says the LORD,
I will answer the heavens
and they shall answer the earth.
(Hosea 2:21)

Our faith tells us that our ability to be faithful to God comes from his fidelity to us. The voice of the church on this sometimes is lost when the culture seems to speak louder. The culture gives us a picture of God that is ambiguous. An influential *Time* cover story in April 1966 asked, "Is God Dead?" Certain opinion-makers inside and outside religion said, "Yes." The discussion was mainly about the existence of God but also about the relevance of religion. If God is dead, he certainly can't be faithful to us in any meaningful sense.

Years later, on October 5, 2009, the Jesuit weekly *America* published a cover story that asked, "Is God Back?" In one sense the answer is no, since he never left us. In another sense the answer is yes, since there is a revival of faith among communities of believers who are responding to God's presence. Our faith is a gift from a living and loving God who lavishly tries to reach us and does so with persistent fidelity. The issue is greater than arguing the existence of God; it is a celebration of a God of love who tries all kinds of ways to touch us. God not only exists, God wants to be present to us. This truth is beautifully illustrated by Holman

Hunt's painting *Christ, the Light of the World*, in which Jesus is insistently knocking at a door that symbolizes our hearts.

IS GOD DEAD?

How is God faithful to his many promises to us? The risen Jesus promised the apostles, "And remember, I am with you always, to the end of the age" (Matthew 28:20b).

At Sinai God formed a solemn covenant with the Israelites and promised he would never break it. When God renewed that promise to David and his descendants, he used strong words:

> I will establish his line forever,
>   and his throne as long as the heavens endure.
> Once and for all I have sworn by my holiness;
>   I will not lie to David. (Psalm 89:29, 35)

Yet there are a number of cases in which God seems to have withdrawn his promise. On Good Friday 1990, I preached on the Seven Last Words of Jesus in St. Thomas More church in New York City. I came to the fourth word, in which Jesus cries, "My God, my God, why have you forsaken me?" (Psalm 22:1). Is it possible that God would abandon his beloved Son?

I was moved to recall the *Time* cover story, with the fire-red letters asking "Is God Dead?" flared out against a black background. I reminded my listeners that the article reported that numerous scholars claimed that religion had lost its power to give meaning to life in a secular culture. Secularists claimed that God was irrelevant to the modern culture —that the modern world was pushing God off the stage. Some religious bestsellers of the day gleefully cited Friedrich Nietzsche's "Parable of the Madman": "'I seek God.... Whither is God?' he cried; 'I will tell you. We have killed him, you and I.'" Then the madman visited churches, where he sang a requiem for God.

That seemed incongruous to me at the time. Vatican II had just finished its last session, pulsing with new life and hope for the Catholic church and religion in general. Just ten years before, Bishop Fulton Sheen had completed a five-year nationally syndicated program, in which he was the first to preach about Christian values on television. New movements such as Cursillo, Charismatic Renewal, and Marriage Encounter infused religion and the experience of a living God with an enthusiasm that celebrated God's fidelity to us. God obviously was still around.

How then did I interpret the agonizing words of Jesus? Had God actually abandoned his Son? How would that be possible? Was God dead? No and no again. I believe that Jesus, in his human nature, betrayed by Judas and denied by Peter, was abandoned—not by God, but by his disciples and those who mocked him at the cross. In the midst of unimaginable physical and emotional pain, Jesus experienced not only personal rejection but also the universal feeling of rejection and the fear that imminent death produces in virtually everyone.

St. Cyril of Alexandria imagines Jesus explaining what was happening. "I am dying for all. I am dying to give them life through myself. In my death, death itself will die and man's fallen nature will again with me. I wanted to be like my brothers in every respect, so I became a man like you."[1]

If we are rejected, Jesus will be rejected. If we struggle with the trials of life, so will Jesus. If we feel God has abandoned us, Jesus tells of the same experience on the cross. In each case he has won for us the power to see this as a test from God, very much as Job experienced. Christ promised us joy and happiness but also tests of suffering that purify our capacity to be patient, heroic, and faithful.

These difficulties in our faith life are what Jesus meant when he asked us to pray, "Lead us not into temptation." St. Paul explains this prayer in the following manner: "God is faithful, and he will not let you be tested beyond your strength, but with the testing he will also provide the way out so that you may be able to endure it" (1 Corinthians 10:13).

17

Certain people dedicate their lives to God to increase their awareness of God's presence. Then God seems to disappear, so that their love and zeal for him is tested. This happened to the famous, ever-cheerful and smiling Mother Teresa of Calcutta, who remained faithful to God. In the book, *Come, Be My Light*, she is described as living in a spiritual darkness for thirty years, a darkness about which only her spiritual directors knew. During that time, she never stopped thirsting for Christ and yearning that his light would come to her. According to Fr. Benedict Groeschel, the light finally arrived:

> I had the opportunity of offering Mass for Mother Teresa on the day before she returned to India, six weeks before her death. She was a transformed person. I have used the word "bubbly" to describe her on that occasion. As we were leaving, I mentioned to my confrere Father Andrew that she was obviously going through the doors of death while she was still alive. It seemed to me that after thirty years of darkness, she was entering the divine light.[2]

Jesus also received the light at the end. Jesus had quoted the first verse of Psalm 22, a psalm he knew from childhood and was well aware of the final words that announce the "coming of the light": The Father did come to his Son to comfort him in the last minutes of his earthly life.

> From you comes my praise in the great congregation;
>> my vows I will pay before those who fear him
> The poor shall eat and be satisfied;
>> those who seek him shall praise the LORD.
> May your hearts live forever!

> All the ends of the earth shall remember
>> and turn to the LORD;
> and all the families of the nations
>> shall worship before him. (Psalm 22:25–27)

In other words, neither God nor our religion is dead.

Is GOD BACK?

God had not died in the sense that modern culture thought it had. God kept his promise to stay with us during every test our church had known—in vicious attacks from communism, Nazism, fascism, and the trials of two world wars—renewing us after the tumult. God appointed a new pope from Poland, a country where faith was profoundly tested by both Germans and Russians. If any people might imagine God was dead, the Poles could—but they didn't.

During his tenure, Pope John Paul II made a spectacular impact by taking his evangelical message to ninety nations all around the globe. It all concluded with one of the most riveting and inspiring funerals the modern world has ever seen. Who could have imagined that America, with its principle of separation of church and state, would send three presidents who came and bowed in respect to the coffin of John Paul?

Add to this picture the powerful witness of Mother Teresa waking up millions to the needs of the poorest of the poor. A pope and a nun confounded all the prophets of doom, who said there was no hope for mankind. Pope John XXIII asked us to ignore such prophets. John Paul and Teresa showed us how to do it.

The America cover story I mentioned earlier, titled "Is God Back?" supported the view that God is very much alive. The red letters of the question imposed on a black background deliberately repudiated Time's report on secularity's deposing of religion. The story is based on Austen Ivereigh's interview of John Micklethwait. Together with Adrian Wooldridge, Micklethwait wrote a book titled, God Is Back: How the Global Revival of Faith Is Changing the World. Ivereigh argued that authors have rejected the secularization thesis that modernity causes the doom of religion, saying, "It is not true that as the world becomes more modern, it becomes less believing. It was never true of the United States—a rather large exception—but now it turns out not to be true almost everywhere."[3] The article contends that in modernized nations, faith flourishes where there is freedom from state control and subsidies.

Churches lose their dynamism when they are established and funded by the state. Micklethwait is amazed "by the level of defeatism among the Anglicans and thinks the Church of England is increasingly recognizing that establishment is a golden noose around its neck."[4] He says that Pope Benedict recognizes the same problem in the German Church tax, which according to Micklethwait "is an enormous funding engine that eviscerates churches as much as it keeps them afloat."[5] Among all the churches Micklethwait has studied, he claims that Catholicism "starts from an incredible advantage," despite recent scandals. He claims that it is multinational and goes so far as to say it is "the General Electric of the religious world" because of its omnipresence and because it has absorbed the "acids of modernity."[6]

What I liked best about the interview was the perspective on the durability of faith in God not *despite* the growth of modern cultures but actually *because* of the possibilities of religious freedom and the value of choice and commitment that can come with it. I also was interested in Micklethwait's observation that the academic community in large part missed this development by assuming that religion was in retreat and that secularity would prevail and replace religion. He argues, "What happened was that the sociology profession carried on writing books that took as their starting point that the world was becoming more secular.... They set out to examine the consequences of that, rather than examine the premise."[7]

Is God back? Actually, he never left. Why not? Because he loved the world so much he gave us his Son to redeem it. And the Son loved us so much that he sent the Holy Spirit to revitalize our faith in God, to lift the hearts of millions of Christians on a global scale. Every time a thousand people close the door to God, the Spirit opens three thousand windows to Christ. To some this may look like a comeback, but the Son of God every day tirelessly knocks at the doors of millions of hearts. "Listen! I am standing at the door, knocking; if you hear my voice and open the door, I will come in to you and eat with you, and you with me" (Revelation 3:20).

The artist Holman Hunt dramatized those words in his much-beloved painting, *Christ, the Light of the World*, to which I alluded earlier. He portrayed the Risen Lord wearing a white robe. On his head is a crown of thorns in memory of the Passion. In his left hand is a lantern. It is night. His right hand knocks at a door that is covered with vines. There is no knob or keyhole. The door can only be opened from the inside. Christ will not force his way in. A faithful God humbly waits at the door and hopes to be invited into our hearts. The Holy Spirit nudges, doesn't force, us to open our hearts to Christ. God never sleeps. Love never tires. The Spirit never rests.

What looks to some like the death of God could be the decline of faith in our everyday life. What appears to be God abandoning us may well be our giving up on him. What causes us to complain that God has lost interest in us often depends on our strange ability to close our ears to his word, to shut our eyes to his enticing beauty, to padlock the entrance to our hearts so we cannot receive his love. In these situations, God's fidelity is matched by our infidelity.

WHAT THE OLD TESTAMENT TELLS US ABOUT GOD'S FIDELITY TO US

In the previous part of this chapter I looked at examples of Christ's faithfulness to us. Examples of fidelity to God abound in the Old Testament, too. For instance, before the biblical David became a great king, he was a shepherd who loved to play music and compose poetry, gifts that initiated the psalms. Alone with his sheep in the night on a Judean mountainside, he felt the loyal presence and protection of God. After a rainstorm he gazed at the rainbow and thought of God's abiding fidelity, remembering that the Lord said to Noah, "I have set my bow in the clouds, and it shall be a sign of the covenant between me and the earth" (Genesis 9:13). David matured with the blessed assurance that he was loved by a God who kept his promises. David strummed his lyre and sang songs of praise to God's fidelity.

In the centuries that followed, David's songs comforted many a band of pilgrims traveling to Jerusalem's temple, tented for the night in the midst of threats from thieves and robbers. A restless sleeper could look out of the tent and see the protective presence of a guard on the hill near the campsite, silhouetted with his spear against the moon. Is the guard asleep? Is God? Even if the sentry slumbered, God did not. The pilgrim could take heart from David's song.

> I lift up my eyes to the hills—
>   from where will my help come?
> My help comes from the LORD,
>   who made heaven and earth.
>
> He will not let your foot be moved;
>   he who keeps you will not slumber.
> He who keeps Israel
>   will neither slumber nor sleep.
> . . .
> The LORD will keep you from all evil;
>   he will keep your life.
> The LORD will keep
>   your going out and your coming in
>   from this time on and forevermore. (Psalm 121:1–4, 7–8)

The faith David had in God's trustworthiness continues to quicken the hearts of all of us in our journeys of faith. We learn from our prayer and our experiences that God keeps his promises. He introduces into a world of frail commitments the ideal of fidelity. God painted a rainbow in the sky to assure us he would always love us without reserve. That visual aid teaches us about God's faithfulness and invites us to practice fidelity in return.

St. Thérèse of Lisieux reached a point in her life where she understood that God's love never left her, even when she had no immediate sense of its presence. She said she felt like a ball that a child throws into a corner. Just as a child knows where the ball is, so God always knew where Thérèse was. She was so convinced of God's fidelity to her that she returned the compliment of sworn loyalty to God: "I have never refused the good God anything."

Human patience with others' difficulties and follies tends to wear thin, however. Too many disappointments sometimes cause us to give up our efforts to improve ourselves and the lot of others. We "burn out" in our fervor. God's patience with human weakness is limitless. He does not tire or burn out. On the contrary, God "burns up" with the passion of loyalty to his friends. And every human being on earth is God's friend to whom he pledges fidelity. Listen again to David:

> The LORD is my light and my salvation;
>   whom shall I fear?
> The LORD is the stronghold of my life;
>   of whom shall I be afraid?
>
> . . .
>
> For he will hide me in his shelter
>   in the day of trouble;
> he will conceal me under the cover of his tent;
>   he will set me high on a rock.
>
> . . .
>
> I believe that I shall see the goodness of the LORD
>   in the land of the living. (Psalm 27:1, 5, 13)

The biblical concept for the Lord's fidelity is *covenant*, a term that talks of a loving agreement in which trust and fidelity are of the essence. In a sense, covenant is the only "gentlemen's agreement" in history where one partner, God, has never gone back on his pledge. In the troubles of life we may find it hard to be loyal to God. It should help us to recall— as in the story of Christ's Passion—that God put up with a great deal to keep his promises to us. In Christ he became one of us to prove how much that pledge meant to him. And remember that pledge is in our best interests, for God's motivation is one of pure love for us. God does not use us to satisfy some divine egoism, nor does he manipulate us as though we were puppets. God likes us and wants us to have the truest kind of personal happiness possible.

When Scripture gets down to business about promises and loyalty, it zeroes in on Mount Sinai, where God entered into a covenant with Israel. We tend to concentrate on the delivery of the Ten Commandments as the essence of that scene, but it is better to begin with the promise of God that precedes the giving of the commandments. Hear again the words of the promise:

> Then Moses went up to God; the LORD called to him from the mountain, saying, "Thus you shall say to the house of Jacob, and tell the Israelites: You have seen what I did to the Egyptians, and how I bore you on eagles' wings and brought you to myself. Now therefore, if you obey my voice and keep my covenant, you shall be my treasured possession out of all the peoples. Indeed, the whole earth is mine, but you shall be for me a priestly kingdom and a holy nation. These are the words that you shall speak to the Israelites." (Exodus 19:3–6)

Nothing has ever stirred the Hebrews as much as their religious experience at Sinai, though the crossing of the Red Sea is equally compelling. At Sinai, a whole people felt God's presence and wrote into their memories his unforgettable promises. So important was that "wedding day" for God's people that heavenly fireworks accompanied the event, as recalled in both Exodus and Deuteronomy:

> Now Mount Sinai was wrapped in smoke, because the LORD had descended upon it in fire; the smoke went up like the smoke of a kiln, while the whole mountain shook violently. (Exodus 19:18)
>
> [You] approached and stood at the foot of the mountain while the mountain was blazing up to the very heavens, shrouded in dark clouds. (Deuteronomy 4:11)

At Mount Horeb, Moses encountered a bush that burned but was not consumed. At Sinai the people beheld a mountain that was on fire but in no way consumed. In their desert marches they had often beheld God lead them in a pillar of cloud or a column of fire. Sometimes they felt his presence in a dense, dark cloud in deep darkness. God told them to expect this: "I am going to come to you in a dense cloud, in order that the people may hear when I speak with you and so trust you ever after" (Exodus 19:9).

The drama of a firestorm at Sinai was the external symbol of a profound meeting between God and his people. God had spent a long time training them for this hour, ever since the day he touched the heart of Abraham and talked to him about the promises of a people beloved of God and numerous as the stars in the sky and the sands by the sea.

Now God was ready to make perfectly clear to Israel the extent of his love and the absoluteness of his pledge to be faithful to them. Lest they should have any doubts, he reminded them of his many acts of love for them—how he bore them up eagle's wings and brought them to this place. Basically he was saying, "I have always loved you. Trust me. I promise you I will always be faithful to you. I want you to be faithful to you. Believe in love." Caught up in the splendor of that moment, they could easily have sung the Carl Gustav Boberg hymn so familiar to us, "How Great Thou Art."

O Lord, my God, when I in awesome wonder
Consider all the works thy hands have made.
I see the stars, I hear the rolling thunder,
Thy power throughout the universe displayed.
Then sings my soul, my savior God to thee,
How great thou art! How great thou art!

Normally, only an individual has such an ecstatic experience of God. At Sinai a whole community found itself enchanted by God's presence and bewitched by his beauty. Isolated mystics have written accounts of meetings with God; here an entire people leave us a record of an exalted hour of their history. Not only Jews look to Sinai to recall the solidity of God's promises, but Christians as well. Sinai has engraved its message on the memory of the Judeo-Christian peoples, a message of divine faithfulness. We find our response to that event in Psalm 95:

> O come, let us sing to the LORD;
>> let us make a joyful noise to the rock of our salvation!
> Let us come into his presence with thanksgiving;
>> let us make a joyful noise to him with songs of praise!
> . . .
> For he is our God,
>> and we are the people of his pasture,
>> and the sheep of his hand.
> . . .
> O that today you would listen to his voice! (Psalm 95:1–2,7)

Subsequent history was to show that God lived up to his promises and that his people broke theirs again and again. It was up to the prophets to touch people's consciences and call them to a renewed commitment in loving fidelity to one another and to God. The prophet Hosea gives us the story of a man who lived in a memorable and inspiring manner the covenantal message that he preached.

Hosea married a woman named Gomer. After she bore her first child, she grew restless with life at home. She began to have love affairs and bore two children from these adulterous unions. Hosea showed patience with Gomer and forgave her infidelities. He raised the children as his own and did not divorce her as the customs of the time permitted. Unaffected by Hosea's forgiving love and showing no regrets for the shame she brought to him, Gomer finally walked out, became a temple prostitute, and ultimately drifted into slavery to a desert chieftain.

Gomer symbolized the recurrent failure of God's people to remain faithful to their covenant with God. They often lapsed into idolatry and resorted with prostitutes in pagan temples. In modern terms, they frequently succumbed to the low moral standards of the pagan culture in

26

which they found themselves. Through all this, God never abandoned his people. Through the ministry of the prophets, God found people whose personal integrity preserved the ideal of marital fidelity and faith in God's promises. Hosea was such a person. Gomer's repeated betrayals and her abandonment of her family for the service of the temples of Baal could easily have embittered Hosea so he could have lost all love for her. Instead, his disappointments nourished in his heart an understanding of God's forgiveness. The Lord of Sinai had endured a thousand betrayals from his people. Instead of gathering before the ark of unconditional love, many of them trooped to pleasure temples and adopted the standards of casual commitment and temporary relationships. As Hosea was vulnerable to Gomer's rejection, so also was God subject to Israel's repudiation of the covenant.

The best cure for betrayal is a healing love from the heart of the betrayed. The effective healing of the hurt inflicted by the unfaithful arises from the balm of forgiveness in the soul of the innocent partner. Loving fidelity is healing response to thoughtless infidelity. Loving forgiveness is the cure for heartless rejection. Jeremiah poses the question:

Is there no balm in Gilead?
   Is there no physician there?
Why then has the health of my poor people
   not been restored? (Jeremiah 8:22)

Hosea's answer is yes. There is always a healing balm in God, ready to soothe and renew a love relationship that has died. Hosea was ready to reach out to Gomer: "Come back to me with all your heart. Don't let fear keep us apart." Despite all that Gomer has done to him, he continues to offer her his love once more. When Gomer is sold into slavery to a desert tribe, Hosea finds out where she is and goes to see her. He asks her to come back to the vineyards she has known and the children she bore. He assures her that she could respond to him as in the first innocent days of their marriage. He convinces her that there is still a chance for a lasting union.

The text of Hosea records none of Gomer's words, perhaps because her experience of such generous and heartwarming love left her speechless. She was healed and forgiven and, after so long a journey, brought to her true home. Hosea perceived the religious meaning of his marital experience as a symbol of God's dream for his people. In the hour of his supreme happiness, Hosea sings a second wedding song to his battered mate. The music that soars from the garden of this old couple echoes the sentiments of God for Israel: "I will make you lie down in safety. And I will take you for my wife forever; I will take you for my wife in righteousness and in justice, in steadfast love, and in mercy. I will take you for my wife in faithfulness; and you shall know the LORD" (Hosea 2:18–20).

IN THE PRESENCE OF AN ANGEL

A famed twentieth-century journalist, Malcolm Muggeridge, journeyed from agnosticism to Catholicism near the end of his life. He testified that his meeting with Mother Teresa in the slums of Calcutta marked a turning point in his commitment to Christ. The following interview was his first report about Teresa.

"Do you do this every day?"

"Oh, yes," she replied, "it is my mission. It's how I serve and love my Lord."

"How long have you been doing this? How many months?"

"Months?" said Mother Teresa. "Not months, but years. Maybe eighteen years."

"Eighteen years!" exclaimed Muggeridge. "You've been working here in these streets for eighteen years?"

"Yes," she said simply and yet joyfully. "It is my privilege to be here. These are my people. These are the ones my Lord has given me to love."

"Do you ever get tired? Do you ever feel like quitting and letting someone else take over your ministry? After all, you are beginning to get older."

"Oh no," she replied, "this is where the Lord wants me, and this is where I am happy to be. I feel young when I am here. The Lord is so good to me. How privileged I am to serve him."

Muggeridge later said, "I will never forget that little lady. The face, the glow, the eyes, the love—it was all so pure and so beautiful. It was like being in the presence of an angel. It changed my life. I have not been the same person since." Eventually he wrote a bestseller about her, *Something Beautiful for God.*[8]

CONCLUSION

I began with the question "Is God dead?" because if he is then his promise to remain with us is not possible. I developed this point in the story of my Seven Last Words sermon and the fourth word, Christ asking God why he has forsaken him. I used the image of a *Time* magazine story that probed the supposed death of God but whose real issue was the assumed victory of a secular culture over religion. This appeared strange in the light of the enthusiasm engendered by Vatican II and movements such as Marriage Encounter and Cursillo.

Next I cited the *America* article, "Is God Back?" which argued modern culture that allows freedom of religion, choice, and commitment actually favored faith; it is only when states control religion that faith loses favor. The second half of this chapter provided the context for God's promises through the covenants from the Old Testament. I illustrated this with the David story, the Sinai event, and the Hosea forgiveness narrative. Scripture's constant testimony returns again and again to celebrate God's fidelity to us.

For Personal Application

1. Why are experiences of God's fidelity important for my own commitment to keep my promises?
2. How aware am I that Jesus knocks at the door of my heart and asks me to open it? How do I respond?
3. How important is it for me to associate with people who are faithful to their commitments?

For Group Discussion

1. How challenging do you find the culture's opposition to faith?
2. If someone asked you for ways to maintain your faith commitment in our secular culture, how would you respond?
3. In reading the examples from the Old Testament—the David story, the Sinai event, the Hosea story—what thoughts went through your mind? What would you do about it?
4. What did Jesus mean when he said, "My God, my God, why have you forsaken me?" When do you experience spiritual aridity?

Scripture Meditation

Let love be genuine; hate what is evil, hold fast to what is good; love one another with mutual affection; outdo one another in showing honor. Do not lag in zeal, be ardent in spirit, serve the Lord. Rejoice in hope, be patient in suffering, persevere in prayer. Contribute to the needs of the saints; extend hospitality to strangers.

Bless those who persecute you; bless and do not curse them. Rejoice with those who rejoice, weep with those who weep. Live in harmony with one another; do not be haughty, but associate with the lowly; do not claim to be wiser than you are. Do not repay anyone evil for evil, but take thought for what is noble in the sight of all (Romans 12:9–17).

PROMISES

I pledge to be faithful to God by:

_____

_____

_____

_____

_____

_____

_____

_____

_____

_____

_____

_____

_____

CHAPTER THREE

BE FAITHFUL TO YOUR REAL SELF

This above all, to thine own self be true;
And it must follow, as the night the day,
Thou canst not then be false to any man.
William Shakespeare, *Hamlet*

WHAT IS THE TRUTH ABOUT BEING HUMAN?
The answer to this question is manifold. Scripture tells us that being human is to live up to being an image of God. "So God created humankind in his image, in the image of God he created them; male and female he created them" (Genesis 1:27). Our human dignity comes from God.

Being human not only originates with God, it also means having a capacity for finding fulfillment in longing for God, as in this psalm:

My tears have been my food
day and night,
while people say to me continually,
"Where is your God?" (Psalm 42:3)

Our true self comes from God and wants to return to God.

The first chapter of the *Catechism of the Catholic Church*, titled, "Man's Capacity for God," opens with this profound truth about each of us. God created us in such a way that only in him will we find real personal fulfillment, truth, and happiness. Our human dignity rests on the fact that we are called to communion with God. The invitation to be friends with God begins the moment we come into being. God created us in an act of love and by that love holds us in being.

Modern culture tries to teach us that we are purely secular people. But God made us essentially religious. Even though many think of America as a secular country, it has more houses of worship per capita than any other industrialized nation. History shows that people have expressed their urge toward God in prayers, sacrifices, rituals, churches, temples, synagogues, and mosques right into the present age.

St. Paul was right when he told the Athenians:

> From one ancestor he made all nations to inhabit the whole earth, and he allotted the times of their existence and the boundaries of the places where they would live, so that they would search for God and perhaps grope for him and find him—though indeed he is not far from each one of us. For "In him we live and move and have our being"; as even some of your own poets have said,
>
> "For we too are his offspring." (Acts 17:26–28)

If this is true, why have so many failed to find God? The reasons are varied. The presence of so many evils in the world overwhelm some and cause them to revolt against the very idea of a God who lets this happen. Religious illiteracy and indifference, which deprive people of even the basic knowledge about God, are other causes. Often wealth so distracts the rich that they rarely think of God. The scandalous behavior of some "believers" drives honest searchers away from religion. Finally, personal sinfulness inclines the sinner to deny the sin, refuse to take responsibility for it, and hide from God.

Then how are we to find the God for whom we long? God reveals himself in three ways:

Through creation: St. Paul tells us that the Creator can be known through the works of creation. St. Augustine puts this truth more dramatically. "Question the beauty of the earth. Question the beauty of the sea.... Question the beauty of the sky.... All respond: 'See, we are beautiful.' Their beauty is a profession. These beauties are subject to change. Who made them if not the Beautiful One who is not subject to change?"[1]

Through the human person: If we think about what we are like, we notice that we want to know the truth and experience perfect beauty. We are attracted to moral goodness. We appreciate our freedom and struggle to maintain it. We are aware of the voice of conscience and try to live by it. We thirst for nothing less than infinite and absolute happiness. These experiences make us aware of our souls and our spiritual nature. The more we realize these facts about ourselves, the more we are drawn to the reality of God.

Through direct revelation: Although the world and human beings are wonderful sources for knowing God, the ambiguity of the signs, caused by human sinfulness, required an explicit and assuring direct Revelation from God about his love for us, his plan for our salvation, and his inner life. In sacred Scripture, as understood within the faith of the church, we have a sure guide to God's extraordinary riches.

Jesus: Our Model and Source of the True Self: As we search for ways to be convinced there is someone noble and attractive deep inside us (a "loveable me"), we would do well to stay in touch with Jesus. If we want to know how to love ourselves properly, we should take a long look at Jesus. Pope John Paul II often asked us to understand ourselves thoroughly—not just in accordance with immediate, partial, often superficial, and even illusory measures of our being—but to address our unrest, uncertainty and even our weakness and sinfulness, with our life and death."[2] Christ reveals to us what it is like to become completely human.

Adam was a human being in the process of growing and searching for ways to realize his inner calling to live like an image of God. To say that

Adam was born in God's image is not to pose a static picture. To be born in God's image means being created with a calling to a lifelong journey toward love, forgiveness, and a reverence for life and creation that is Godlike. In Jesus this process is complete. This is why St. Paul tells the Colossians, "You have heard of this hope before in the word of the truth, the gospel" (Colossians 1:5).

Jesus is more than an example of how to be true to ourselves. He is also "This Tremendous Lover," the title given to him in Cistercian Fr. M. Eugene Boylan's book of the same name. Christ confers on us the creative love that helps our dreams about ourselves come true. We must do more than look *at* Jesus as though we were staring at a masterpiece in a museum. This spectator attitude requires no involvement, no openness to receiving the love that is an absolute necessity for our personal growth.

Jesus calls each of us to a love affair in which we permit him to share himself with us and to allow him—the Word through whom all things were made—to be as creative with our selves as he was with the world itself. Dependence on and involvement with others—Jesus as well as other people—are the real keys to achieving the correct sense of self-worth, a self-image that makes the heart sing. This is the kind of self that makes our fidelity to it so worthwhile.

GRACED INTERDEPENDENCE: AN ACT OF MUTUAL DEPENDENCE

No scene of matched needs surpasses the scene of mother and child on Christmas night. We know Mary's role as a mother, full of fond affection and ready to pour out her love on this marvelous new son of hers. The mother gives; the child receives. And yet the child gives and the mother receives, as well.

I once saw a picture of a lion in cage. Strangely, the lion was crouching in the corner, somewhat subdued. In front of him was a lioness with jaws wide open, apparently roaring at the lion. The caption said, "Even the king needs to listen to the queen."

A working marriage is a portrait of graced interdependence. Movies,

36

plays, and novels never tire of describing the so-called "battle of the sexes," usually with couples before marriage, yet the challenge of inter-dependence is typical of married couples. The couple wants an ideal marriage. Husband and wife may forget that two sinners just wedded. They dream of an ideal relationship but forget how much work, patience, prayer, discipline, and realistic expectations that will require. The old saying is still true for couples: Pray as if everything depended on God; act as if everything depends on you.

I am a fan of Msgr. Charles Pope, a pastor in Washington, D.C.. His website is a treasure of pastoral wisdom, such as I quote here.

> The most dangerous period in marriage is the first five years because that's when the ideal gives way to the real and the real ushers in resentments. Some start looking for a new deal. In the end the key is to accept the real. Now acceptance is not the same as approval or appreciation. Acceptance is serenity about what is, even if there are some things we wish were different. We don't live in the ideal, we live in the real and there is seren-ity and stability in accepting that fact. More marriages might survive if the partners realized that sometimes the better comes after the worse.[3]

Which is the greater gift, strength or dependence? Who is more enhanced by the exchange? The gifts are incomparable, for each needs the other. We pride ourselves on being aggressive in loving another. We tend to forget that the other must in freedom give us a chance to bestow our gift. This becomes remarkably clear at Bethlehem, when the Son of God assumes the helplessness of human infancy. The sheer joy of Mary fussing over her child comes from the fact the child is helpless and needs her so much.

We tend to frown on dependence. Often we are right, if dependence means spoiled people who simply want us to wait on them. We harbor a proper dislike for those who sit around moaning that the world owes them a living. Pretended helplessness based on laziness is simply an ego trip.

Yet there is legitimate dependence based on a real sense of need. When we are honest enough to admit our limits and look to others for aid, our vulnerability invites others to confer their love on us. A stern form of independence only keeps others at arm's length from us.

In the manger at Bethlehem, Jesus displayed the dependence that opened him to the gifts of Mary and Joseph, the shepherds, and the Magi. This healthy dependence continued during his childhood, his adolescence, and his quiet years at Nazareth. He was not afraid to welcome the love and affection he received from Mary, Joseph, and others. It was his way of learning about love. Yet we must add that in his twelfth year he reminded his parents that he was also receiving love from his Father. To his human parents he said, "Why were you searching for me? Did you not know that I must be in my Father's house?" (Luke 2:49).

BEAUTY AND THE BEAST

Insights into the true self come to us from soul-shaking words such as the televised sermons of Bishop Fulton Sheen. Others do this through sublime works of art or by the boundless patience of a scientist.

Visualize the ceiling of the Sistine Chapel in Vatican City on which Michelangelo depicted God's creation of Adam. God rides a cloud toward Adam. Weak and dreamlike, Adam stretches out his arm toward God and extends one finger to touch God's finger. In the painting, Adam's finger falls slightly short of touching the finger of God. Between God's finger and that of Adam is narrow and empty space. Yet, as millions of tourists and pilgrims have seen, flowing into that space is the creative life of God that surges into Adam. Michelangelo spent four years on his back to decorate the ceiling of the Sistine Chapel and to give us that breathtaking moment from the book of Genesis. He painted the human body in its glory; it seemed filled with the divinity approaching Adam. Four centuries later this scene still causes us to admire what God

BE FAITHFUL TO YOUR REAL SELF

did for us and what we are meant to be.

Travel now from the sixteenth-century chapel to the twentieth-century game preserves of West Africa, where animal researcher Dian Fossey had been observing gorillas, their habits, and their mannerisms. After waiting a very long time, she wanted to see if a gorilla would come near her peacefully. She gently coaxed one of them like someone in a park luring a squirrel with a nut. A four-hundred pound ape, a real King Kong, came near her. He picked up her pencil. She touched him softly. And then he reached out his paw, capable of bending iron. He tapped her so gently she scarcely felt it. This was more than beauty taming the beast. It is a moment of communion with creation. She proved that the normal ferocity of a gorilla could be met with human, nonthreatening behavior. Like Francis of Assisi, who addressed creation with the simplicity of a dove, Dian Fossey has walked that path with the cunning of a scientist.

Michelangelo brought the heavens close to the earth with his frescoes on the ceiling of the Sistine Chapel. Dian Fossey brings the earth close to the heavens in her godlike approach to the fiercest beast. It is in their common humanity that both achieve a miracle. They tell us that in our quest for feeling good about being human, we come to be more relaxed about our divine destiny and our common heritage with creation. We need not be ashamed with our fellowship with the animal world nor vain about our intimacy with God. In our humanity we stand in the clearing where the Creator and the creature unite.

Shakespeare's *Hamlet* gives us the lines to fit this vision.

What a piece of work is man!
how noble in reason! how infinite in faculty!
in form and moving, how express and admirable!
in action how like an angel! in apprehension how like a god!
(*Hamlet*, II, 2)

The psalmist is even more lyrical:

39

When I look at your heavens, the work of your fingers,
  the moon and the stars that you have established;
what are human beings that you are mindful of them,
  mortals that you care for them?
Yet you have made them a little lower than God,
  and crowned them with glory and honor. (Psalm 8:3–5)

Despite these uplifting passages, there is much about us that we could lament. Sin and evil are too near the bone to ignore easily. However, if Jesus thought nothing of us he would never have come to redeem us. If he had so low an opinion of us that he concluded we were a hopeless lot, he would have ignored us and given up the project. Yet Jesus could look at our warts and follies and our cruelties and deadening sins and see something more than the quintessence of dust. He saw our potential for holiness and greatness, for generosity and heroism, and precisely because of all that, he resolved to give us a chance to live up to these possibilities. As the perfect combination of idealist and realist, Jesus knew he could save us if we accepted his gifts of reconciliation, forgiveness, a second chance to start over, and the hope for eternal life and joy.

MY IDENTITY: AN IMAGE OF GOD

What does it mean to be an image of God?

I have a mind that can know the truth, including the ultimate truth of God and the realization that God is truth.

I have a will that can love the good in the world and the absolute good that is God.

I have received the gift of freedom. I am free to do what I should and not just whatever I please.

I have been wounded by original sin. This means I have a difficult time knowing the truth and must struggle for it. I notice a conflict in my will. I often choose what I shouldn't— and fail to choose what I should. I am inclined to evil in the exercise of my freedom.

I have new life in the Holy Spirit, due to my baptism and my participation in the sacraments. These graces help me not just to "be" an image of God, but also to "act" as God's image and overcome the difficulties posed by original and actual sin.

I am destined for the life of glory in heaven. It is because I am an image of God that I even have the possibility of happiness. The capacity to know and love in a properly free manner opens me to the only permanent source of joy, an enduring relationship with God.

CONCLUSION

Faithfulness to the true self is based on the teaching of Scripture that God created us in his own image. God endowed us with human dignity. God also created us with a capacity to long for him, a drive to our ultimate destiny in eternal life. The self comes from God and is meant to return to God. This is the dynamism of being human. This is not an easy calling.

God has revealed his plan for the true self through creation, through the qualities of the human— especially in hearing the voice of conscience—and finally through direct revelation. While not everyone can have rigorous calling like martyrdom or poverty, everyone will experience challenges in being faithful to the truth about being human. Jesus said it openly: "If any want to become my followers, let them deny themselves and take up their cross daily and follow me" (Luke 9:23). The life of Jesus is a picture-perfect illustration of the true self in action. Jesus shows us how to be completely human and to walk the path to eternal joy. Through the imitation of Christ, the grace of God, and a dialogue of dependence with each other, we can nourish and mature the true self we have received.

FOR PERSONAL APPLICATION

1. When you hear the word "self," what comes to mind?
2. What is the advantage of seeing the self as an image of, and the inner longing for, God?
3. How does this vision of self affect your moral behavior?

FOR GROUP DISCUSSION

1. How widespread is the cultural view of the self as an image of God and a process of longing for God? How does this compare with your own position?
2. What lesson comes from the examples of Michelangelo and Dian Fossey?
3. What would we mean when we say that Jesus shows us the meaning of a true self?

SCRIPTURE MEDITATION

So then, putting away falsehood, let all of us speak the truth to our neighbors, for we are members of one another. Be angry but do not sin; do not let the sun go down on your anger, and do not make room for the devil. Thieves must give up stealing; rather let them labor and work honestly with their own hands, so as to have something to share with the needy. Let no evil talk come out of your mouths, but only what is useful for building up, as there is need, so that your words may give grace to those who hear. And do not grieve the Holy Spirit of God, with which you were marked with a seal for the day of redemption. Put away from you all bitterness and wrath and anger and wrangling and slander, together with all malice, and be kind to one another, tender-hearted, forgiving one another, as God in Christ has forgiven you." (Ephesians 4:25–32)

PROMISES

I pledge to be faithful to my true self by:

_____

_____

_____

_____

_____

_____

_____

_____

_____

_____

_____

_____

_____

CHAPTER FOUR

Stay Faithful to Your Friends

If a man does not make new acquaintances
as he advances through life, he will soon find himself left alone.
A man should keep his friendships in constant repair.
Samuel Johnson

I grew up as an only child in the Rittenhouse Square section of central Philadelphia. There were no children nearby for me to play with on the street where I lived. But, I found my friends—many of whom I still consider friends—just three blocks away near my parish church, St. Patrick, at 20th and Rittenhouse. The Moccia family lived right next to the church, and their home became a gathering space for the scattered neighborhood youth. Of the four Moccia children, Bobby was closest to my age, and we began a friendship that has endured the many tests of time. Gradually a "gang" was formed that included Ed Cusack, Mike McHugh, Jack Lenahen, Jack Senske, Mike Flynn, George McGoldrick, and others who came and went. Around the park were apartment houses, and Bobby and I had odd jobs such as walking dogs and running errands for those residents. Several of us went on to South Catholic High School, staffed by the Norbertine fathers. I was the first to graduate, and I joined the order in Wisconsin. I would reunite briefly with my friends on short vacations, but little by little our paths separated as my priesthood duties kept me in Wisconsin. None of us kept in touch through letters.

Bob married and raised three children. He became a successful manufacturer's representative supplying heavy-duty kitchen equipment to schools, hotels, and hospitals. In 1966 I moved to Catholic University in Washington, D.C., as a visiting professor, which led to my getting a doctorate in religious education and starting an office in that field for the National Catholic Educational Association. This all meant that I would be in that city for twenty years.

It also gave me a chance to reconnect with Bob and his family. Like all real friendships, there was little need to fill in the gaps. We met again as though we had never parted. There was a comfort level that tied us together with signals, memories, tough times, and joys that eventually shaped our personalities. Old friends are often the best friends.

At the end of this period I returned to my abbey in the Midwest for eight years and then came back to the D.C. area to work with the Paulist fathers in evangelization. I also continued my friendship with Bob. That endured after my appointment as a professor at Blessed John XXIII National Seminary in Weston, Massachusetts, not far from Boston. By this time Bob invited me regularly to Thanksgiving with his family and that of his second wife, Ria.

He started a custom that we have followed ever since, gathering the surviving friends from our childhood for a lunch at Popi's in South Philadelphia on the day before Thanksgiving. We acquired another friend, Joe Gorman, who was a sports star in our youth and a bit older. Now we talk about our doctors and pills as well as old times. Yes, there are walkers and canes. It is an easy meeting—funny, serious, joyful, sad, and grateful for what has endured. There is a forgiving quality in such friendships, a shared amusement at our frailties, and a pride in the goodness we see in each other. They took pride in my priesthood and attended my golden jubilee in St. Patrick Church.

Throughout my life I made many other friends, especially with families I came to know in my various ministries. The community life in the Norbertine Order is ready-made for friendships and general willingness to accept one another. I have a number of close friends within the order whom I treasure. During our training years we heard every week the Rule of St. Augustine read at table while we silently ate our meals. His opening words urged us to live a community ideal. We prayed:

Let us love God above all things, dearest brothers, then our neighbor, for these are the chief commandments given to us. The first purpose for which you have come together is to live in unity in the house and to be of one mind and heart on the way to God.

A FAITHFUL FRIEND

Scripture records many stories of faithful friendships. The story of Peter's friendship with Christ is one such example. Peter loved Jesus, and he knew that Jesus loved him. Peter was clumsy in human relations. A fighter by nature, he did not understand Christ's submission to death. Peter wanted a more "macho" Jesus. Yet when courage was needed, Peter failed the test and Jesus did not. Jesus faced up to the most dangerous people in town, but Peter could not even stand up to a group of strangers. Just when his best friend needed him, Peter lost courage.

While Jesus was on trial before the religious court, Peter was outside warming himself by the fire. A maid recognized his Galilean accent and said, "You also were with Jesus the Galilean." In front of the others, he said, "I do not know what you are talking about." Another woman saw him and also accused him of being on Christ's side. Peter took an oath and declared "I do not know the man!" Then others repeated the accusation, to which Peter replied with curses and swearing, "I do not know the man." The cock crowed. He left the courtyard and wept bitterly (see Matthew 26:69–75).

Despite his cowardly behavior, deep down Peter never lost his friendship with Jesus, and Jesus never lost his affection for Peter. After Easter, Jesus came to Peter and gently teased out of this normally inarticulate fisherman a threefold declaration of love (see John 21:15–17). Peter is not accustomed to speaking of love openly, but Jesus helps him heal the wounds of his triple denial by the triple affirmation of love. Three times Peter said firmly, "Yes, I love you, my Lord." Then Jesus commissioned him to the powerful ministry of leading the body of Christ to the world.

Gone now is all his timidity about faith and love. The first twelve chapters of the Acts of the Apostles describe a Peter who goes to jail, is scourged with whips, and is fiercely attacked by the enemies of the faith. When warned he must stop preaching and healing in the name of Jesus, he and John forthrightly vowed, "But Peter and John answered them, 'Whether it is right in God's sight to listen to you rather than to God, you must judge; for we cannot keep from speaking about what we have seen and heard'" (Acts 4:19–20). Eventually Peter goes to Rome and is martyred for the faith.

The Easter scene at the beach disclosed a vision of leadership that is founded on love given by the Holy Spirit (Romans 5:5) and loyalty between the leader and the apostle. It flowed from an adult view of friendship that commanded trust and respect. Jesus did not ask for apologies about the denials, but he took a public risk to ask for Peter's vows of love. The creases around Peter's eyes told the tale. Peter caught the precise dignity of the moment—a fresh opportunity to be born again.

He put behind him his failures and disappointments. He had confessed his sins with tears. This Easter dawn at the beach where Peter had launched so many fishing trips—in his homeland of Galilee—signaled the beginning of a new creation, a new Peter on whom the Holy Spirit at Pentecost would put the finishing touches of his sublime calling.

Peter would never be a St. John, taking spiritual flights like an eagle. He could not dream of matching the eloquence of the literary genius of St. Paul. He had a humbler form of genius, the capacity to become the first chief shepherd of the church. He remained lovingly faithful to Christ until his martyrdom in the circus of Nero some thirty years later.

If you visit St. Peter's Basilica in Rome, be sure to gaze up at the words carved in stone at the base of the dome. The Latin quotes Christ's declaration to Peter: "You are Peter and upon this rock I will build my Church and the gates of hell shall not prevail against it" (see Matthew 16:18). There, within one of the grandest churches in Christendom, is the grave of St. Peter. The body of the fickle yet finally totally loyal fisherman of far-off Galilee rests here.

So on earth is fulfilled the special promise Jesus made to Peter: "I will give you the keys of the kingdom of heaven"(Matthew 16:19). This is likely why popular images have Peter at the pearly gates checking out all those who arrive for their eternal reward. The friendship between Peter and Christ was a rocky road that eventually became a smooth path to God.

A Faithful Woman Friend

Another Scripture story illustrates the grounding of kept promises. Our common sense and powers of reason tell us, "Yes, promises are important. They give us a hold on reality and make life satisfying." But our powers of reason can also be used to rationalize any situation, to explain away the need to keep a promise. So we must look beyond ourselves, to the power of the Holy Spirit, for an unshakable vision of promises kept.

In our last chapter we looked at the scriptural version of fidelity to promises through the theme of covenants. God has promised to love us, care for us, and always forgive our failings so we can return to him. The whole biblical storyline is a celebration of God's trustworthy fidelity to his promises to us.

A special example of this is the story of Ruth. It begins with a farm family from Bethlehem facing economic depression due to widespread crop failures. Naomi and her husband Elimelech conclude that they must leave home and migrate with their two sons to Moab, a neighboring country whose prosperity offers them the chance for survival. They worry about being aliens in a different culture and religion. Nonetheless, Moab it must be. The people prove to be prosperous and friendly, and they make the strangers from Bethlehem feel at home. The

Moabites sell them land, help them to succeed, and eventually arrange for the marriage of the two sons to Moabite women, Orpah and Ruth.

Ten years of happiness pass. Then an epidemic strikes the family, killing off the male members and leaving three grieving widows. Naomi feels frightened and alone. She does not want to be a burden to her two daughters-in-law; they are still young enough to seek new husbands. Naomi is homesick. Times are better back in Bethlehem, and she has relatives there who would probably take her in. She could do some kind of work to survive. She resolves to go home.

Naomi says good-bye to her daughters-in-law, thanking them for their care and wishing them happiness and peace in the homes of their new husbands. Dutifully the daughters protest that they should go back with her to Bethlehem. Naomi appreciates their offer but reminds them she has no more sons. They must look out for their own future and find husbands in Moab. Orpah kisses Naomi farewell and goes away.

But Ruth feels a bond of affection for Naomi. She holds the aging Naomi in her arms and utters a canticle of friendship that ranks with the world's immortal poetry:

> Do not press me to leave you
> or to turn back from following you!
> Where you go, I will go;
> where you lodge, I will lodge;
> your people shall be my people,
> and your God my God.
> Where you die, I will die—
> there will I be buried.
> May the Lord do thus and so to me,
> and more as well,
> if even death parts me from you! (Ruth 1:16–17)

Small-town gossip assailed the two women upon their return to Bethlehem. Some claimed that Naomi first abandoned her homeland

and now has returned with a "pagan" like Ruth. Naomi grows bitter over this hostility, but Ruth is not shaken. She has made a promise of fidelity to Naomi and is determined to stay with her. To keep them from starvation, Ruth goes out to the barley fields to pick up the leftovers behind the reapers.

One day she attracts the attention of a rich farmer, a middle-aged man named Boaz. It is a case of love at first sight. He gives her permission to reap in the best fields and invites her to have lunch with him at noon. That evening, she tells Naomi about her good luck. Naomi praises God for this happy turn of events and devises a plan to bring Boaz to marry Ruth. When Boaz settles down to sleep, Ruth must go to his tent, turn back the covering at his feet, and lie there till Boaz tells her what to do.

Blatant seduction? Not in this case. Boaz is touched that she would place herself in such a vulnerable position but more satisfied that her real purpose was to seek him as a husband. So Boaz marries Ruth. When they come together as husband and wife, the Lord enables her to conceive and bear a son, Obed. Obed became the father of Jesse, who sired King David, of whose family was born Jesus Christ, the savior of the world.

In God's providential plan, Ruth's fidelity not only brought comfort and peace to Naomi in her final years, it also introduced Ruth into the genealogy of Jesus. Ruth's fidelity associated her with the ultimate meaning of the covenantal promise: that God is not the God of just one human tribal family, but of all the tribal families and nations on earth. This story is an early hint of the universality of God's plans for the whole world.

St. Paul: It Wasn't Easy to Be His Friend

Some friendships begin well enough but do not last, either due to volatile temperament or policy disagreements. Try being a close friend to a man of volcanic emotion such a Paul of Tarsus. At least in his early years, he exemplified the old adage about the saints: It is one thing to live with the saints in glory; to live with them on earth is another story.

After his conversion, Paul spent several years in the desert prayerfully contemplating his new vocation from God to be an apostle to the gentiles. When he was ready to be a missionary, he traveled to Jerusalem for Peter to confirm him in his preaching and give him a job. Barnabas eased the way for Paul, but Peter saw that Paul was still too controversial and tended to upset matters too much. Peter judged that Paul needed more seasoning in solitude and prayer. Much to the credit of both men, Paul accepted Peter's instruction to go to Tarsus and await the call.

Four years later, the call came. Barnabas brought Paul the news, and they planned the mission journey. Barnabas's fellow missionary, John Mark, joined the other two as they sailed away. Things did not go well between Paul and John Mark. Paul was annoyed with John Mark's refusal to head for the rugged mountains, and he was impatient with John Mark's homesickness. When John Mark eventually sailed home, Paul thought of him as a deserter.

When a second missionary journey was being planned, Barnabas suggested bringing John Mark. Paul blew up. After this disagreement, Paul and Barnabas parted company (see Acts 15:37–39). In Paul's mind, none of this was personal. The importance of the Christian mission was at stake. He mellowed later and invited John Mark to join him, but he did not include Barnabas. As the following passage shows, Paul's passion for the Gospel did not give him time to work on his friendships:

> I thank my God every time I remember you, constantly praying with joy in every one of my prayers for all of you, because of your sharing in the gospel from the first day until now. It is right for me to think this way about all of you, because you hold me in your heart, for all of you share in God's grace with me, both in my imprisonment and in the defense and confirmation of the gospel. For God is my witness, how I long for all of you with the compassion of Christ Jesus. And this is my

prayer, that your love may overflow more and more with knowledge and full insight. (Philippians 1:3–5, 7–9)

JONATHAN'S STUBBORN FIDELITY TO DAVID: FROM A TREATISE ON SPIRITUAL FRIENDSHIP

by Blessed Aelred, Abbot

Even when the king pronounced the sentence of death upon David, he did not desert his friend. *"Why should David die? How has he sinned? When he risked his life and killed the Philistine, you rejoiced. Why should he die?* So maddened was the king at these words, he tried to pin Jonathan to the wall with his spear, heaping upon him further abuse and threats: *Bastard son of a wayward woman,* he screamed. *I know well that to your undoing, and that of your shameful mother's, you love him. . . . As long as the son of Jesse lives, your kingdom shall never be established.*

Who would not be moved to envy by these words? Whose love, whose favor, whose abiding friendship would not be corrupted, weakened, and destroyed by such an utterance? But in his great love, this young man kept faith with his friend. He was steadfast in the face of threats, unmoved by insults; forgetting renown, he thought only of service. He spurned a kingdom for the sake of friendship. *You,* he said to David, *will be king and I will be second to you.*[1]

CONCLUSION

Paul's story should comfort all of us who have ups and downs with our friendships. Lovers' quarrels do not just happen between lovers; they occur among friends as well. "Hug and make up" is as much a part of being a friend as it is of being a lover. In fact, the distinction between a lover and a friend is not always clear, since love is the substance of the relationship in each case. Friends can be infuriating at times, but so what? No one is perfect, least of all our humble selves. An old Irish adage says it best: "It is better to quarrel than to be lonely."

So it is with friendship's pitfalls, as we saw in the friendship between Jesus and Peter. Friendships can be rocky roads pitted with betrayal, made smooth with loyalty, and ever a challenge. They range between sorrow and a good laugh. Human resiliency makes it possible for the rubber band of commitment to stretch surprisingly far. Fidelity to friendships is one of the nicest things that can happen to us—and this history of human encounter shows that it occurs frequently. The friendship between Ruth and her mother-in-law is one of the most beautiful in the Bible and literature as well. Ruth pledged her friendship and sacrificed her homeland and all that was emotionally dear to her to remain faithful. Friendships are rarely perfect. As with all serious relationships, there are angry moments, slights, betrayals, even spite—yet true friends can overcome these unfortunate tests.

While I cited St. Paul's friendship struggles, I also need to highlight his magnificent description of love (*agape*) in 1 Corinthians 13. Paul also offered an incomparable explanation of the Spirit's gift of faith for all relationships in his letter to the Romans, and in everything he wrote he reminded us of the centrality of Jesus Christ in all our thoughts, words, and deeds. These were the tools that made him a saint. These are rivers of wisdom for our own spiritual lives.

For Personal Application

1. Think of the history of your friendships, the ups and downs. What have you learned?
2. Augustine says that God sends us our friends. What does that mean for you?
3. How did you react to the Peter, Ruth, and Paul stories?

For Group Discussion

1. Augustine believed that we do not choose our friends; God selects them for us. What is your experience?
2. Some people like to have cliques that exclude others. How does this fit with the ideal of *agape* or universal love of others?
3. Augustine thought that friendship began with the Spirit pouring divine love into our hearts and ending with Christ's kingdom—a community of friends loving one another. How does this compare with what you know?

Scripture Meditation

And when he comes, he will prove the world wrong about sin and righteousness and judgment: about sin, because they do not believe in me; about righteousness, because I am going to the Father and you will see me no longer; …

When the Spirit of truth comes, he will guide you into all the truth; for he will not speak on his own, but will speak whatever he hears, and he will declare to you the things that are to come. He will glorify me, because he will take what is mine and declare it to you. All that the Father has is mine. For this reason I said that he will take what is mine and declare it to you.

"A little while, and you will no longer see me, and again a little while, and you will see me."(John 16:8–10, 13–16)

PROMISES

I pledge to be faithful to my true self by:

_____

_____

_____

_____

_____

_____

_____

_____

_____

_____

_____

_____

CHAPTER FIVE

STAY FAITHFUL TO YOUR COMMUNITIES

No man is an island...
Each is a piece of a continent...
Therefore, send not to know
For whom the bell tolls,
It tolls for thee.
John Donne

When John Paul II visited Poland after his election as pope, he brought home to the world the importance of fidelity to our communities: family, country, and church. His homecoming was like a parish picnic on a scale so grand one could hardly believe it possible in our lonely, doubt-ridden times. Millions converged upon the pope: grandmothers in their babushkas, babies held up for blessings, excited teens, coal miners, and dignitaries all heartily singing, *Christus Vincit* ("Christ conquers"), an exuberant hymn of faith in God and the indomitability of the human spirit.

On Pentecost evening, John Paul was in Gniezno, Poland, where Christianity was established one thousand years ago. He spoke of Polish Catholic culture, urging people to stay faithful to the traditions of their country and church and that they should be nobly proud of it and pass it on to future generations.

One standard of fidelity to a community is the realization of how much you miss it when you can't be there. In this spirit, the pope led the people in singing the mountain ballad, "Don't you miss your country, your fields and pastures, your valleys and streams?" As they wept and sang with John Paul, they knew he sang of a man called to duty in Rome.

Fidelity to community is a mysterious and profound form of loyalty to country, church, parish, religious order, school, or fraternal organization. The military has a strong pull of commitment, especially for career officers such as the Pacific hero of World War II, General Douglas MacArthur. His farewell address to the cadets at West Point is filled with emotion:

> The shadows are lengthening for me. The twilight is here. My days of old have vanished, tone and tints. They have gone glimmering through the dreams of things that were. Their memory is one of wondrous beauty, watered by tears, and coaxed and caressed by the smiles of yesterday. I listen vainly, but with thirsty ears, for the witching melody of faint bugles blowing reveille, of far drums beating the long roll. In my dreams I hear again the crash of guns, the rattle of musketry, the strange, mournful mutter of the battlefield.
>
> But in the evening of my memory, always I come back to West Point.
>
> Always there echoes and reechoes: Duty, Honor, Country.
>
> Today marks my final roll call with you. But I want you to know that when I cross the river, my last conscious thoughts will be of the Corps, and the Corps, and the Corps.
>
> I bid you farewell.[1]

Listening to a soldier celebrate the tug of fidelity to his military school touches a responsive and universal value. Fidelity to a particular community draws us out of ourselves. It reminds us of the need to be faithful and concerned about the one family to which everyone belongs—the human family.

The intermediate communities that nourish this spirit—parishes, schools, clubs, nations—liberate us from the narrow cell of ourselves. They turn our gaze outward toward the pageant of people, the brawling mass of humans, who delight and outrage us, frustrate and charm us, yet invite us to take part in the great drama of living.

OUR PARISH CHURCH: A HOME FOR FAITH

It is popular today to speak of church as a community and not think much about the physical building. The emphasis on people is essential, but the building has its truth as well. Dwellings, whether divine or human, possess a kind of holiness. People whose homes have been burglarized describe the experience as a kind of very personal violation. More than the vandalism or what was stolen, the knowledge that uninvited strangers could run loose in one's "sanctuary" stirs up wrath about the invasion of our sacred space. Even though a dwelling is made of brick and stone, wood and steel, it becomes personal because it belongs to us. We endow it with our personalities; we may talk about our "personal blessing" of the space. Home acquires a kind of holiness because of the affection we bring to it. When someone lives many years in one dwelling, it takes on a distinct personal character.

This kind of mystical communion between ourselves and our homes is echoed in our parish churches. Divine and human presence conspire to make that space sacred and give the community a feeling of belonging. God is present in our parish churches for daily celebration of the Eucharist as well as at weddings, funerals, confessions, baptisms, confirmations, anointings, parish picnics, choir practices, religious education, faith formation, RCIA, marriage preparation, and all kinds of other meetings. Just read your Sunday parish bulletin to scan the range of activities in the life of the parish.

The hundreds, even thousands, of religious events in a parish church over the years—sometimes centuries—penetrate the very stones of that church, much like the sacred oil that anointed its stones when it was consecrated. The love affair that occurs when God and his people meet in outpourings of prayer and faith endows the parish church with an aura, an atmosphere of awe and reverence. The very building assumes a kind of sacramental character. It has a lived-in look that reflects the parishioners' acts of faith and Christ's holy presence in the Blessed Sacrament.

Old parish churches assume the feel of living history. Famous churches such as New York's St. Patrick Cathedral are our local churches writ large. They provide the assurance that the life of faith is worthwhile. The parish church works like a good poem, evoking the memory of the faith of people from the past and drawing the people of the present into the living chain of believers.

Some years ago I visited an old Catholic village church in Scotland near the highlands. In the vestibule of the church, I saw an oval picture of a deceased pastor. Underneath his picture was the simple inscription, "In loving memory of Father Angus Campbell, who served this church faithfully for forty-three years." Old people walk by that picture and recall what he meant to them when they were young. Middle-agers barely remember him, but they intuitively take power from his memory and see themselves as part of something bigger and comforting in an environment of faith in God. The children look up and run quickly, but already they are acquiring a sense of belonging to the church.

During my annual visits to my hometown of Philadelphia, I never fail to visit the parish church of my childhood, the previously mentioned St. Patrick. I always go to the east entrance to the lower chapel, where several former pastors are buried. Among them is Fr. Thompson, whom I remember from childhood. He was tall and heavy but cheerful, and he loved to stand at the back of church greeting people after the Masses and evening devotions, a custom that was new for Catholics in those dark days of the Depression. He was well known and loved for his heartfelt devotion to the needs of the poor, who made up the majority membership of the parish. My prayer for him at his parish grave is one of thankfulness for what he meant to me and my family. Though I have lived elsewhere for most of my life, I treasure the connection he gives to me on those occasions.

The Human Factor

Parish life is as perfect or imperfect as the people who belong there. This will always be so in a sinful world or, more positively, among believers who struggle and stumble through their faith journey. That is why reconciliation rooms beckon us to forgiveness. That is why Jesus in the Blessed Sacrament invites us all for a dose of divine love. That is why every Mass offers us the medicine of mercy and the promise of self-betterment. That is why the Stations of the Cross remind us of the road of tough love to which Jesus summons us. That is why statues of Mary, Joseph, the parish patron saint, and other saints greet us with their desire to intercede for us. That is why the colorful biblical people in the windows celebrate for us the final victories of grace in their lives. There is hope.

In any attempt to create fidelity to parish community, however, you must be prepared to cope with the inevitable folly—and sadly, the rudeness—of some community members, a few of whom may be parish leaders. The participatory style encouraged in parish life today accentuates the possibility of an unpleasant experience. The involvement of more and more people in the active life of the parish also extends the chances for personal conflict. It grows harder to avoid people who do not listen, who want their own way, who wish to impose some kind of liturgical interpretation of social behavior on others while forbidding them to have their say.

On the other hand, the community emphasis attracts many dynamic, creative, talented, and noble-minded people to active participation in parish life. These people generate enthusiasm for the faith and improve the quality of loyalty to the parish. In scriptural terms, they are the leaven that allows the population to rise to a common goal. These are the dedicated individuals who sponsor converts and support the excellent "Catholics Come Home" program that has done so much to reverse the long trend of Catholics drifting away from the parish. In many positive ways, they supply the energy that might be lost due to the shortage of priests and nuns—God love them—who did so much in the past to create a dynamic American church.

By tapping the remarkable gifts of parishioners for the good of the community, Catholic life is quietly undergoing a renewal that makes the future look appealing and encouraging. This healthy development comes from the fact that gifted parishioners act from their belief in the truths of Jesus as one who loves them with a boundless affection. The very walls of the church are like a voice of divine love that taps their volunteerism in the knowledge that love is multiplied in the giving. Every Sunday the miracle of the loaves happens again. From five loaves Jesus multiplied enough to feed thousands of people. The bread was multiplied in the giving. The living bread of the Eucharist is offered again and again. In practical terms, talented participation in the life of the parish is life-giving because it proceeds from Christ's love.

DEVOTIONS, ANYONE?

In October 2009, a beautiful reliquary containing some bones of St. Thérèse of Lisieux toured England, drawing more than eighty thousand people to see it and touch the oval glass surrounding the box. People are surprised that this would happen in Protestant England, where Catholics number six million in a sea of sixty-five million people. Even the venerable Anglican York Cathedral hosted her relics. Part of the success is the enduring affection for St. Thérèse, whose teaching about accessible holiness continues to have wide appeal. Her "little way" of doing ordinary acts with great love for God and people remains a captivating ideal for everyday spirituality. She makes it possible for Catholics to seek God's presence in material signs. In the Old Testament, miracles were worked through the cloak of Elijah and the bones of Elisha. Luke's Gospel reports the story of a woman who is healed by touching the hem of Christ's robe, and Acts notes that even Peter's shadow healed people. Material things can be signs of God's healing presence.

Devotional practices provide ways to deepen people's faith. Making the Sign of the Cross with holy water when entering the church, genuflecting to the Blessed Sacrament, saying a decade of the rosary while waiting for Mass to start, lighting a candle at a shrine after Mass, reading a devotional litany after Communion, leaving a rose at Mary's statue—these are all small acts of devotion that stimulate faith in God's presence and trust in God's mercy and love. Holy cards, with pictures of Mother Teresa and favorite saints and with prayers on the reverse side are making a huge comeback. These are tools for personalizing our relationships with Jesus, Mary, and the saints. Scapulars, medals, incense, and relics have been popular with Catholics for centuries dating back to the Roman catacombs, when the faithful began honoring the bones of the martyrs. Other rituals include the ashes on Ash Wednesday and palms at the beginning of Holy Week and—most tenderly—kissing the cross on Good Friday. Pilgrimages to Lourdes, Fatima, Guadalupe, and the Holy Land are occasions for refreshing and revitalizing faith in the providence of God and the value of the intercession of our Blessed Mother on behalf of our needs.

Scott Hahn's book, *Signs of Life: 40 Catholic Customs and Their Biblical Roots*, makes the case that our seemingly little devotions help people to appreciate the great mysteries of our religion. In an interview with the newsweekly *Our Sunday Visitor*, Hahn explained why devotions are so essential to Catholic life: "Catholic life is caught more than it is taught. What I mean is that you assimilate the truths of Faith more by what you do together with other Catholics, experiencing the grace of Christ in the family of God, than by sitting in a classroom and taking it in through lectures, or by listening to homilies and talks on CDs."[2]

MASS APPEAL

In the spirit of the Christophers' motto, "Don't curse the darkness; light a candle," Archbishop Timothy Dolan wrote a letter to the faithful of New York, urging them to return to Sunday Mass. As part of the letter, he offered the faithful who keep the Sabbath holy these tips on what to say to those who make excuses for not going:

—"Sunday is our only free time together." (Great! What better way to spend time than by praying together at Mass?)

—"I pray my own way." (Nice idea. But odds are, you don't.)

—"The sermon is boring."(You may have a point.)

—"Until the church makes some changes in its teaching, I'm staying away." (But don't we go to Mass to ask God to change us, not to tell God how we want him and his church to change to suit us?)

—"Everybody there is a hypocrite and always judging me." (Who's judging whom here?)[3]

CONCLUSION

I have traveled to a great many countries around the world and lived in Belgium for a year of study. While I enjoyed the trips, I always liked getting home to America. Hearing "The Star-Spangled Banner" at sports events always touches me, and in the weeks after 9/11 I teared up every time I sang "God Bless America." I know that patriotism undergoes ups and downs and is manipulated by certain politicians and opinion-makers, but I believe that love of country is a good thing.

The natural beauty of America from coast to coast is breathtaking. The open hearts and wallets that respond to disasters at home and abroad is always uplifting. The freedom of religion—despite some secular rants about freedom from religion—remains a unique and successful experience envied around the world. The respect for the armed forces that defend our freedom is nurtured in our hearts even amid disputes from time to time about how they are deployed.

These thoughts support our fidelity to America. Faith, family, and flag are the basic cultural groundwork for the American dream. But the incessant noise—from TV, newspapers, texting, Twitter, Facebook, blogs, YouTube—can be an unfiltered roar from a culture that demands to be heard no matter how superficial the comment, how disturbing to common sense and conscience, how sacrilegious, how corrupt. This is not meant to be a prophecy of doom; it's just a wake-up call for us to access our faith resources and to call for a time-out so we can come to our senses.

For our church, American culture has become a special challenge. In the next two chapters, which discuss marriage, family, priesthood, and celibacy, I will reflect on the obvious issues that require a vigorous and responsible reply from the Catholic community in union with other people of goodwill. Much of what I write has been said by many more eloquent voices, such as the late Fr. Richard John Neuhaus, who led people of faith to take their proper place in the public square. Archbishop Charles Chaput has done the same in his excellent book, *Render Unto Caesar*, as has Supreme Knight of the Knights of Columbus Carl Anderson in his book, *A Civilization of Love: What Every Catholic Can Do to Transform the World*.

As my Irish mother used to say, "The situation is serious but not desperate."

Our church has much depth and millions of people who can bring the teachings of Christ in a dynamic and responsible way to curb the excesses of the culture and build on the principles of America's Founding Fathers. Let us share with our fellow citizens the richness of our faith in Jesus Christ, the moral ideals that our faith offers, and the wholesome lifestyle that Christianity has brought to cultures throughout the ages—Greece and Rome, barbarian tribes in Europe, the era of

Enlightenment, and now a secular philosophy that promotes a world without God and a life without standards. In the bones of Catholicism is a storehouse of acquired wisdom. Yes, we are not angels, but neither are we devils. We are flawed humans who love our country a lot!

FOR PERSONAL APPLICATION

1. Are you active in your parish? What are your thoughts about it?
2. How does parish life enhance your faith and family life ?
3. What improvements could you contribute to your parish?

FOR GROUP DISCUSSION

1. How would you assess your contributions to your parish life? Discuss the section in this chapter about the impact of the church building on your faith and attachment to the church at large?
2. How do you handle the conflicts, pettiness, and negativity that can arise within parish life? How do you benefit from the outstanding leaders—priests, laity, nuns, deacons—who influence your parish?
3. Why is devotional prayer effective?
4. How do you feel about the closing words on the love of country? How would you express your love of country?

SCRIPTURE MEDITATION

The gifts he gave were that some would be apostles, some prophets, some evangelists, some pastors and teachers, to equip the saints for the work of ministry, for building up the body of Christ, until all of us come to the unity of the faith and of the knowledge of the Son of God, to maturity, to the measure of the full stature of Christ. We must no longer be children, tossed to and fro and blown about by every wind of doctrine, by people's trickery, by their craftiness in deceitful scheming. But speaking the truth in love, we must grow up in every way into him who is the head, into Christ,...(Ephesians 4:11–15)

PROMISES

I pledge to be faithful to my church and country by:

_____

_____

_____

_____

_____

_____

_____

_____

_____

_____

_____

_____

CHAPTER SIX

STAY FAITHFUL TO YOUR MARRIAGE

A successful marriage must be rebuilt every day.
Anonymous

In the film Fireproof, *Captain Caleb Holt, a firefighter, works by the axiom:* "Never leave your partner behind." In the fading embers of his marriage, however, he and his wife Catherine live by their own rules. After seven years of marriage, Caleb and Catherine have drifted so far apart that she wishes she had never married. Each partner is leaving the other behind. Neither understands the pressures the other faces, he as a firefighter and she as the public relations director of a hospital. They have no children. They live parallel lives. Catherine has fallen in love with a doctor at the hospital; Caleb is in love with his $25,000 boat. They argue constantly over their jobs, finances, housework, and outside interests. After one of their shouting matches, Catherine demands a divorce.

This wakes Caleb up and moves him to visit his dad for help to save the marriage. His dad gives him a little book, *The Love Dare*, a forty-day guide for reviving a marriage. Each day proposes a dare, accompanied by a Scripture passage and some specific advice. Caleb accepts the challenge and proceeds to do what he can to save the marriage. Over the next twenty days he gives Catherine flowers, cooks her a candlelight supper, cleans the house, and uses a number of other ways to try to win her heart back. She rejects his overtures with increasing contempt. He

69

doesn't know why this isn't working and becomes depressed and angry. He goes back to his father, describes his frustrations, and tells him he is giving up the idea.

His dad invites him to take a drive to a nearby woodland where there is a clearing for meditation. Several tree trunks are arranged in a semicircle and smoothed for sitting down and facing a large wooden cross. The dad encourages Caleb to confide his list of disappointments, which he then delivers with passion and anger. Caleb concludes with, "Catherine has refused every offer of love.... How can I love her when she constantly rejects me over and over and over again?"

His father moves over to the cross and quietly rests his head against the wood. He says that in his marriage he had to be changed by Christ. He needed to learn to love God and to receive his forgiveness. He now understands that God loves us even when we constantly reject him. He looks at his son and reminds him that God's standards are higher than human ones; that's why Jesus said that hatred was as bad as murder, that lust was as bad as adultery.

These words, spoken as he leans on the cross, begin to touch his son. Little by little, Caleb becomes aware that for twenty days he was basically trying to force Catherine to be thankful, loving, and forgiving. Force is fatal. Only love—humble, forgiving, and repentant, coming from the spirit and nourished by prayer—has any hope of opening the door of her heart. To hear his father confess that he had to let Jesus transform him, that he needed to use that divine power to save his own marriage, was a witness that moved Caleb to faith and conversion.

The moral of the story is, "Never leave your partner behind." (For the rest of the story, you will have to see the film.) Our reflection continues this theme of facing up to the challenges of marital fidelity. There are many beautiful ways to sustain marital fidelity. Out of that abundance of wisdom, I present you a mosaic of five guidelines:

1. KEEP YOUR PROMISES

At the heart of your wedding are the promises you make to one another. The priest says, "Since it is your intention to enter into marriage, join your right hands and declare your consent before God and his church." Then the bride and groom exchange promises: "I,[name], take you, [name], to be my wife/husband. I promise to be true to you in good times and bad, in sickness and in health. I will love you and honor you all the days of my life." Receiving their consent, the priest says, "You have declared your consent before the church. May the Lord in his goodness, strengthen your consent and fill you both with his blessings. What God has joined, no one should divide. Amen."

This is a tender moment in the lives of couples. The marriage promises are a form of lasting love the couples make to each other. Love is an emotion, but it is more than that. Love is a decision that may or may not be sustained by feelings. On the wedding day, emotion is close to the surface. It makes the promises clear and simple. Ten years later, we hope the love will be deeper and the feeling more mature. Everyone dreams that the promise to be bonded to each other has come true.

Couples should never forget that broken promises mean broken hearts. Broken promises cause pain. A good deal of the pressure points in married life can be traced to the failure to keep the promises. The church teaches that marriage is forever. Our culture used to agree that was a good idea. The magazine *Ladies Home Journal* has been asking the question each month for decades: "Can this marriage be saved?" In the past, the answer was usually yes. These days, I am not so sure.

The Bible's consistent teaching about love is that it is meant to last forever. St. Paul writes:

Who will separate us from the love of Christ? Will hardship, or distress, or persecution, or famine, or nakedness, or peril, or sword?... For I am convinced that neither death, nor life, nor angels, nor rulers, nor things present, nor things to come, nor

powers,... nor height, nor depth, nor anything else in all creation, will be able to separate us from the love of God in Christ
Jesus our Lord. (Romans 8:35, 38, 39)

Keeping promises requires intimacy not just with each other, but also
with the fidelity of Christ. Jesus is the third party in a Christian marriage.
That is the point that Bishop Fulton Sheen made in his excellent book,
Three to Get Married. To be convinced that marital fidelity is possible,
people need to experience it, both from a relationship with Christ and
with the witness of married people who have stayed the course. To
know that Christ will never break his promises to us makes it easier to
believe that spouses can keep their promises to each other.

Some cynical opinion-makers today have said, "No one can hope to
keep their marital promises for life. You can stay together until growth
do you part." This assumes that mutual self-development will automat-
ically cause the breakup of the marriage. But we believe the marital
promise includes the hope that the relationship will be beneficial to both
spouses. The spouses should promise to draw out of each other the
beauty, wonder, and glory God planted there.

A loyal promise is an act of trust—the very basis of a civilized society
and a strong church. Keep your promises. Jesus kept his to you. Life
experience will bear this out.

For Catholics, marriage is a sacrament. It is a loving, faithful, permanent union of husband and wife. It mirrors Christ's sacrificial life for us,
and through marriage we also experience his grace. The Catholic tradi-
tion has always understood marriage as a natural relationship, as well.
Marriages in every faith matter—to God, children, each other, and the
community. Marriage helps create and care for the next generation,
helping to satisfy men's and women's deep longings for connection with
each other and children's longing to know and be known by their own
mother and father. Marriage works by fostering commitment, trust,
fidelity, and cooperation between the sexes.

2. Remember That Marriage Matters

According to Bradford Wilcox and others at the Institute for American Values, marriage matters for twenty-six different societal reasons. In their published study they cite seven major issues facing society as a consequence of the breakdown of the institution of marriage. Their research affirms the importance of marriage for the common good. Here are some of their conclusions:

Marriage reduces the risk of poverty for children and communities. Most children whose parents don't get or stay married experience at least one year of poverty.

Fatherless households increase crime. Boys whose parents divorced or never married, for example, are two to three times more likely to end up in jail as adults.

Marriage protects children's physical and mental health. Children whose parents get and stay married are healthier and also much less likely to suffer mental illness, including depression and teen suicide.

Men and women who marry live longer, healthier, and happier lives. On virtually every measure of health and well-being, married people on average are better off than their single counterparts.

Living together is not the same as marriage. Married couples who cohabit first are 30 to 50 percent more likely to divorce. People who just live together do not get the same boost to health, welfare, and happiness, on average, as spouses. Neither do their children. Children whose parents cohabit are at increased risk for domestic violence, child abuse, and neglect. Children born to parents who were just living together are also three times more likely to experience their parents' breakup by age five.

Parents who don't get or stay married put children's education at risk. Children whose parents divorced or never married have lower grade point averages, are more likely to be held back a grade, and are more apt to drop out of school. They are also less likely to graduate from college.

When marriages fail, ties between parents and children typically weaken. Adult children whose parents divorced are only half as likely to have warm, close ties to both their mother and their father. For example, in one large national survey, 65 percent of adult children of divorce reported they were not close to their fathers (compared to 29 percent of adults from intact marriages).[1]

3. FEED YOUR LOVE

I heard a story about two brothers, one of whom was a bachelor and the other was married with a large family. They jointly owned and worked a wheat farm and a mill for making grain. They invested equal amounts in their business and agreed to split the profits fifty-fifty. At harvest time each brother divided the day's gathering of wheat evenly.

One day the single brother thought to himself, "I don't think it's fair to divide the grain evenly. I have only myself to think of. My brother has a wife and children to look after." So each night he secretly took some of his wheat to his brother's grain bin so that he would have more wheat for his family.

Another day the married brother reflected, "I don't believe it's just to divide the grain evenly. My wife and I have children to provide for us when we grow old. What will my brother have for security when in his advanced years?" So every night he secretly carried some of his wheat to his brother's grain bin.

Then one night the brothers met each other carrying wheat to each other's granary. They laughed when they realized what was happening and hugged one another with love. A legend says that God witnessed their love and said, "This is a holy place, the kind of place where I would build a shrine."

From time to time, couples have a chance to review the state of their marriage. They might approach the review as if marriage is a human contract. In that case, they could be cordially formal and declare, "We are in this marriage on a fifty-fifty basis." That may have some advantages, but it will never satisfy the generosity that arises from selfless love. Their marriage needs to be more than a contract. It must be a covenant of love.

Just as the brothers affectionately thought of each other's needs, so the couple should identify their mutual needs and learn to appreciate them with a loving response. God will smile when he sees that kind of love in a marriage and say to himself, "This is holy ground. I will make a shrine and live here." God will live in their united hearts as in a temple and spur them to even bigger acts of thoughtfulness.

4. WORK TO MAKE YOUR MARRIAGE GROW

Make time for each other. At the wedding there was the first blush of love, the time when the seed was sown. Real love takes time to grow and mature. The couple might plant a tree in the yard or a seed in some potting soil in their apartment. Let them observe the slow growth of the plant and the miracle of nature teaching them how love grows slowly but surely. Of course, this will be even truer when their first baby is born and they witness the process of growth.

In their busy married lives, the spouses should never be clockwatchers when it comes to caring for their relationship. They will benefit from sharing peaceful hours of affection and understanding. It is a gift to behold when they frequently pause to meet and be with each other. This not only deepens their feelings for one another, it protects them from ever becoming strangers under the one roof. Marital love is worth risking big chunks of time to make it happen.

Appreciate each other. Keep in touch with words. There are times for silence, but there are also times for words—words that heal, that cheer, that resolve the differences that arise. Words that are sweet nothings, and words that must create understanding after the "fighting words." Don't let, "It goes without saying" be part of your married life. Affection needs to be shown in words as well as deeds. There is no need to give a speech or utter elegant phrases. A simple, "I'm proud of you" or "I love being with you" can say it all.

Stay close. This is so easy to do. Touching is a warm way to express love. Never give that up. Hugs and kisses are powerful expressions of feelings and visible signs of caring.

So take time. Appreciate each other. Stay close. Married love is too valuable to lose. Besides, God is looking for a new shrine where he can be at home.

5. TRUST EACH OTHER

Pope John XXIII liked to give this advice to parents: "See everything. Correct a little. Forget most." His relaxed point of view hit the right balance between a restrictive and a permissive position. He called for large doses of trust in relationships between parents and children as well as between spouses.

Perhaps you have seen the poster that shows a child letting a bird fly away. The caption reads, "Let the bird go. If it comes back to you it's yours. If it doesn't, then it was never yours in the first place." When you trust someone you use a long leash, because you are confident that you need not control the person as a proof of love. As a grandmother might say to her grandson, "Don't hug the kitten too tightly. It might scratch you and then run away."

Trust is never a matter of control, of hugging too tightly. There must always be a space to grow. Anyone who has ever planted a cluster of evergreens knows that as the trees grow they begin crowding each other. Then you need to thin out the trees, transplanting some so that all have a place for maturing. It is the same with married couples. The reason the spouses treat each other with trust is that they provide space to grow.

The lover and the beloved must never try to own each other as though they were property. Spouses are always people, centers of freedom, and meant to be treated with dignity. Spouses are bound together by love and trust, but the bond must be one in which you "hold the reins lightly."

At the wedding feast of Cana, we watch the relationship of trust between Mary and Jesus. For thirty years, Mary has enjoyed the presence of her son in the home in Nazareth. Now she sees he must go forth to his "hour" or, more aptly, his mission as Savior of the world. Their conversation about the wine shortage conceals the deeper dynamic of trust and challenge as related to the mission. Mary wants her son to begin his hour, even if it means she must let him go and no longer have his consoling presence at home. He seems reluctant to enter the dangerous aspect of his destiny, but Mary entrusts him to his freedom, saying, "Do whatever he tells you."

In the desert, Satan had tempted him to perform a miracle that would make him an "economic messiah." At Cana, Mary calls him to perform a miracle that would reveal his glory, his role as Savior. Satan asked him to abandon his ideals. Mary challenged him to embrace them with decisive action. Satan wanted to control Jesus. Mary trusts that she can let him go and never lose him.

This scriptural event is an image of the trust spouses must embrace. Trust involves (1) letting go of controlling loved ones; (2) giving the beloved the space to mature; and (3) challenging each other to be deeper, more loving, and more concerned.

This is a lesson that will be learned only through experience, trial and error. Recall the old adage, "Good judgment is the product of experience. Experience is the product of bad judgment." Spouses need not be upset by failing from time to time in this adventure of trusting. It takes a lot of time to study and master. Reflect on the example of Mary and Jesus. Rely on Mary's prayers and the graces Jesus can place in your heart. Trust each other humbly, patiently, and joyfully.

How Families Can Practice More Christ-like Behavior in a Modern World

Advertising hits all of us thousands of times a day. A large number of these appeals use materialistic motives to sell products. The more that like-minded families band together to create a Christian counterculture, the healthier our children will be. Here are a few pointers that every family can practice to create a Christ-like alternative:

1. Dress modestly. Clothing makes a statement. If your clothes are intentionally seductive, then you are sending the wrong signals. If you dress modestly, whether formally or informally, then the signal to others is: "I respect myself, and I respect you."

2. Speak with imagination. Virtually every young person is getting a relatively good education today; a great many obtain college degrees, as well. The potential for speaking well is greater than ever and can enhance the human dignity of both speaker and listener.

3. Listen to good music. This can include modern musical forms as well as the classics. Music sends powerful emotional messages. Why not listen to music that is romantic without fostering dehumanizing relationships?

4. Acquire visual literacy. When viewing movies, TV, advertisements, magazines, and websites, keep in mind that there are aesthetic and moral standards that support the values of beauty, truth, and health in all entertainment forms.

5. Save sex for marriage. Virginal purity in both men and women is an attainable ideal. Cultures upheld this standard for centuries, and it can be done again. The ideal has never been perfectly realized, but the support for it makes a great difference for families, society, and the quality of life.

CONCLUSION

The Irish have a ring called the claddagh. On the ring you will find a heart that speaks of love, folded hands that tell of friendship, and a crown that stands for fidelity. The claddagh symbolizes the different facets of a couple's faithfulness to one another. These facets combine into a love that strives to echo God's everlasting love for their lives and their family.

These ideals form a contrast to the story of modern marriage and family that tends to stress the downside—divorce, cohabitation, marital unhappiness, and single-parent families. It would be unrealistic not to acknowledge this. However, the teachings of the church, which I offer you in this book, stand as a remedy to such societal downsides. As Pope Benedict has said on various occasions, "We do not impose our teachings, but we ceaselessly propose them."

The programs, catechisms, and other ways by which the church hopes to overcome what is happening to customary marriage, family, and child-rearing are a part of the solution. We should also acknowledge that there are millions of Catholics who are regular churchgoers, active in their parishes, devoted to their children and grandchildren and each other. There are also thousands of priests and dedicated laity who work in parishes to help the cause and provide the spiritual resources for needed growth in holiness.

That said, we further need to form passionate Catholics, one by one, through conversion, prayer, and penance. We also must continue to grow in faith, hope, love, and courage. Give more attention to individual formation. Trust in the power of the saints. Their example of holiness is inspirational and motivates us to follow them to Christ. Historically, the church has suffered by sin in its ranks as well as persecution from outside. We need to relearn penance and accept purification. Let us make ourselves and every Catholic a radiant presence of the gospel of Christ and the power of the Holy Spirit in the home, family, culture, economics, and politics.

PRAYER FOR MARRIED COUPLES

Father in heaven, you are the author of marriage and you willed that the covenant of husband and wife should reflect the covenant you have established with us. Your beloved Son willed that the covenant of marriage should reflect his own union with the church. In these events the virtues of fidelity and self-sacrificing love are paramount, along with all Christian ideals that ensure the stability of the family and look to the welfare of children. We pray for all the virtues, gifts, and blessings we need to fulfill these Christian ideals of marriage and the family. Amen.

Personal Application

1. How is modesty practiced in your household? What expectations do you have about clothing, music, language, TV, movies, and the Internet? What success stories from other families have been helpful to you?

2. If you were able to create a neighborhood that would support your family values, what would you require? What help would you expect from your parish family? How can the church be your partner in strengthening marriage and family?

3. What is the greatest obstacle to marital commitment today? What is the relationship between self-sacrifice and marriage?

FOR GROUP DISCUSSION

1. What helps you to practice fidelity? Why is family loyalty such an important virtue? What do you see around you that challenges your ability to be faithful to your spouse?

2. What are the benefits of focusing on the ideal side of family life? What do you learn from an honest appraisal of the realistic aspects of marriage and family?

3. What spiritual activities help your family grow closer? How do your help one another to pray? Why is faith a strong bond for your family?

4. If you were to rate yourself on marital fidelity on a scale of one to ten, where would you find yourself? Are you relatively satisfied? What would improve the situation?

SCRIPTURE MEDITATION

When Jesus had finished saying these things, he left Galilee and went to the region of Judea beyond the Jordan. Large crowds followed him, and he cured them there.

Some Pharisees came to him, and to test him they asked, "Is it lawful for a man to divorce his wife for any cause?" He answered, "Have you not read that the one who made them at the beginning 'made them male and female,' and said, 'For this reason a man shall leave his father and mother and be joined to his wife, and the two shall become one flesh'? So they are no longer two, but one flesh. Therefore what God has joined together, let no one separate." (Matthew 19:1–6)

PROMISES

I pledge to be faithful to my marriage by:

_____

_____

_____

_____

_____

_____

_____

_____

_____

_____

_____

_____

_____

CHAPTER SEVEN

BEHOLD, A FAITHFUL PRIEST

The woods are lovely, dark and deep.
But I have promises to keep.
Robert Frost, "Stopping By Woods on a Snowy Evening"

As our church grapples today with vocations to the priesthood, I am reminded of the American nuns of my childhood. From sea to shining sea, they were phenomenal vocation recruiters. Such was my eighth-grade teacher, Sr. Bartholomew Marie. A sister of St. Joseph of Chestnut Hill, Pennsylvania, she was a born teacher. Each hour of the class day she rotated groups—those writing on the board, those standing to recite, those completing a written assignment, those working on a spelling exercise. She was like a symphonic conductor, keeping all of us involved in the adventure of learning. She added an hour to our class day to prepare us for admittance to a Catholic high school, a sacrifice of her personal time and a treasure for us. After lunch every day she took us through a small booklet that was filled with one-liners, brief prayers that we recited so often we had memorized them by the end of the year. I hear them yet and recite them now: "Jesus, meek and humble of heart, make my heart like unto thine." "O Mary, conceived without sin, pray for us who have recourse to thee."

Midway through the second semester, Sr. Bart took me aside and told me she would drill me to prepare me for a spelling competition at the

Jesuit high school, commonly known as St. Joe Prep. A few months later, on a fateful Sunday afternoon, I joined the group of boys at the school. I was one of the last two standing when I was given the word sagacity, which I spelled s-a-g-a-s-i-t-y. As runner-up I did get a half scholarship, but I was still unable to afford the school. I felt sheepish when I rang the convent door to tell Sr. Bart the news. She was disappointed, but she said, "No matter, you will go on to high school, and you will do well."

Many years later, when I was working at the National Catholic Educational Association, I was giving a lecture to a large audience of teachers in Newark, New Jersey. My topic was "Individually Guided Instruction," which I illustrated by telling them how Sr. Bart taught my eighth grade. I had no idea she was in the audience. A group of St. Joseph sisters met me after the lecture and said, "She's here!" And there she was, much I remembered her, tall and matronly. Somehow I felt like a little boy again.

Not long after this, Sr. Bart celebrated her golden jubilee. I planned to attend, but she wanted only her family and the local parish to be there. I sent her one of my books with an inscribed tribute. Her thank-you note was so touching that I taped it on my mirror to remember her in prayer. Her one request I could not forget was, "Father, if possible, would you celebrate the Mass of the Resurrection at my funeral?" I promised her I would, hoping that circumstances would allow. Later, on the feast of St. Bartholomew, Sr. Bart went to God. I had just finished a retreat to our community and was able to celebrate her funeral Mass.

Sr. Bart was one of the countless legendary nuns who make Catholic education such a blessing and success. She was also part of that huge, elite corps of nuns who fostered vocations to the Catholic priesthood. She was always faithful to her vows to her heavenly spouse, Jesus Christ. God sent her into my life, a gift I will always treasure. She helped me know that fidelity to priesthood was possible.

SUCCESSFUL OR FAITHFUL?

In Thomas Kunkel's book, *Enormous Prayers: A Journey Into Priesthood,* the journalist follows twenty-eight modern priests working throughout the United States. One of my favorite stories—and most inspiring and memorable as well—was that of Msgr. Ralph Beiting. Before Beiting became a priest, he, the oldest of eleven children, grew up on a small farm in Northern Kentucky. It was in his early teens he felt the call to priesthood. The bishop at that time found it difficult to get a priest to minister in Appalachia, a mountain paradise inhabited by the poorest of the poor. The bishop began sending seminarians there in the summer so they would get to know the area and be inspired to work with the people. Among them, the young Ralph Beiting saw the needs and thought about helping out. Fortunately, the bishop appointed him to be a pastor there in 1949, the second year of his priesthood. At the time, a quarter of a million people had abandoned Appalachia to find work in the cities so they support their families. The people who stayed behind needed basic necessities—food, clothing, and shelter. They also needed education, training, skills, self-improvement, and ways to make a living where they were. They needed hope. Beiting understood that they needed aid with both the symptoms and the causes of poverty.

Beiting began by begging for food and clothing from the folks back home, but soon he realized his people needed a conversion to self-respect and personal growth, as well as a vision for their future. To face this challenge he created the Christian Appalachian Project. He started a simple newsletter that appealed for funds and other help and, to his amazement, people responded.

Today, Beiting sends out appeals to up to twenty-five million people. In addition to providing summer camps for children, he has established a number of businesses for job creation: a timber company, gardening training, woodworking shop, and dairy farms. He has attracted numerous volunteers as the project has become well known. Beiting goes on occasional speaking tours to spread the news. Many have honored him, including presidents of the United States. He treats these awards as means to a greater purpose. He says the awards are not for him but rather for God.

Without such a spiritual vision, Beiting's approach would not work as well. He recounts the story of a group of people asking Mother Teresa how she felt, knowing that the old people she cared for would soon die, and she had no way to change that. How could she ever feel successful? She answered, "I didn't know I was supposed to be successful. I thought I was supposed to be faithful." That is exactly what Msgr. Beiting believes, too.[1]

Faithful to Celibate Priesthood

The sex abuse scandal has effected a number of changes, among them the Charter for the Protection of Children and a more serious screening of seminary candidates. The formation of seminarians has also been revised, according to Pope John Paul II's apostolic exhortation, *Pastores Dabo Vobis* ("I Will Give You Shepherds"), which includes a fourfold program of theological, pastoral, human, and spiritual training. There is also a deeper approach to celibacy at all these levels. The following pages offer some perspectives on this solemn commitment of priests.

Church law can motivate some priests to lifelong fidelity to celibacy, but this motivation alone may not be enough for many priests. The higher motivation is love of God and, in Christ, the love of people. Such love is always the best reason for fidelity. Nothing makes celibacy more tolerable and durable than the experience of divine affection—the fruit of a prayerful relationship with God. No argument in favor of celibacy and fidelity to it surpasses the promise of knowing that God offers the priest the warmth of his love in turn for a claim on the priest's heart.

Flowing from this logic of love is the motivating force for commitment to friends, communities, and those in need. The celibate priest faces the challenge to fidelity in a number of ways. One is through loving friendships. Think of the saints who were famous for their deep friendships: John of the Cross and Teresa of Avila, Vincent de Paul and Louise de

Marillac, Francis de Sales and Jane de Chantal, Jesus and John.

Celibacy is more than the absence of sex. It is also the presence of love for God and others. Fidelity to God results in fidelity to people. Recall Mother Teresa as she waded into a sea of humanity with her warm smile, caring hands, and healing heart. She was faithful to her virginity, yet she was no "untouchable" as she walked among the poor as a nurse, mother, and woman. She had no fear of physical affection when it was offered for the love of God and the needs of people.

Television brought us hundreds of pictures of Pope John Paul II, a committed celibate, roaming the world, kissing babies, hugging men and women, smiling, shaking hands—with his eyes wide open with delight in the passing parade of humanity. His celibate fidelity was energized by an outpouring of love in a worldwide gesture of affection. This was a constant theme at World Youth Days. When asked what they, the participants of World Youth Day, thought of John Paul they would say, "He is the kindest man I ever saw or met."

Precisely! Celibacy is never meant to generate lonely spinsters or bachelors. Genuine fidelity to celibacy moves the priest toward people, not away from them.

Dorothy Day was a committed celibate for the latter part of her adult life. She lived right in the middle of New York's teeming throngs, begging food and clothing for the poor. She also fought to change the system that oppressed the poor, and she struggled against those who promoted wars. Bound to God by an inexpressible love, Day prophetically revealed the compassion of God. She became one of the most important Catholics in American church history. She valued her celibacy and remained faithful to it because she had fallen passionately in love with God and his poor.

Celibate fidelity flourishes where community life exists and permits the members to grow as prayerful and loving human beings. We can expect a high ratio of celibate fidelity where genuine Christian community serves the celibate members. A community that encourages its members to deal with their relationships openly and honestly is fostering the possibility of long-lasting fidelity. Such communities put a high priority on a prayerful relationship with God.

Celibacy is a way of loving God. The celibate becomes aware of God's claim on the priest's loyalty and affection, a seeming possessiveness that is at first fearful. But soon the celibate finds out that God is no narcissistic devourer of the human spirit. God throws no tantrums when the beloved celibate shows affection for people. In fact, God is delighted, since that is the expected fruit of the consecrated life.

CELIBACY AND SEXUALITY

I have stressed that problems of celibacy are due to the absence of love, not the absence of sex. However, it would be a mistake not to note the role of sexuality in the celibate life. Sex presents challenges for many celibates, not because they lack genital fulfillment, but because they worry about dealing with sexual arousal. Some celibates seem surprised that they continue to have sexual feelings and corresponding physical reactions even after many years of celibacy.

The vow of celibacy does not turn the priest into an angel. Celibates remain human beings with sexual feelings and reactions. A priest will feel attracted to a beautiful woman sometimes as much as noncelibates will. The vow will not erase such emotions. Experiencing sexual temptations is the common lot of people on earth.

What is a celibate to do?

Beautiful ideals are sometimes hard to live up to. Celibacy requires daily attention. Celibates need encouragement from the members of their own community and from the church at large. St. Paul asked the Romans to encourage each other: "For I am longing to see you so that I may share with you some spiritual gift to strengthen you—or rather so that we may be mutually encouraged by each other's faith, both yours and mine" (Romans 1:11–12).

Homilies of encouragement have their place in the church, but how much more persuasive are the words of comfort between friends in the household of the faith! The author of Hebrews writes, "And let us consider how to provoke one another to love and good deeds, not neglecting to meet together, as is the habit of some, but encouraging one another, and all the more as you see the Day approaching" (Hebrews 10:24–25).

Heart-to-heart talks in which we share only troubles, and no one speaks of hope and change for the better, tend to generate despair. Allowing our friends to get something off their chests is fine, but we must do more than that. Even while we lift some burden off their shoulders, we should also find a way to put something hopeful in their hearts. What else would Paul have meant when he wrote, "Therefore encourage one another and build up each other, as indeed you are doing" (1 Thessalonians 5:11).

Prayer, too, is crucial in ensuring the durability of celibate commitment. Prayer, accompanied by spiritual direction and regular confession, is a tried-and-true formula for celibate living. Communal sharing, such as I discussed above, may not intrude into the sacred space of a priest. While that kind of sharing is valuable, so too is the privacy of meeting with a confessor and receiving spiritual direction. Prayer and regular, wise guidance from a trusted priest is very helpful for staying celibate.

From a practical point of view, modesty in dress, especially when on vacation or off duty, is required. Discipline of the tongue, above all the jokes we tell, will help a lot. Avoid the salacious stories and puns that often arouse feelings that should remain dormant. "But now you must get rid of all such things—anger, wrath, malice, slander, and abusive language from your mouth" (Colossians 3:8). Discipline of the eyes, too, has become more important, due to the thousands of unwanted visual images that assail the priest from TV, the Internet, and other technological sources. Pictures not only speak a thousand words, they also creep into our fund of imagining, most of which is better left unseen. Self-denial in these areas will help acquire the virtue of purity that strengthens priestly celibacy.

When Jesus said that some will choose celibacy for the sake of the kingdom, he was teaching the world that consecrated celibacy is a sign that it is possible for human beings to fall passionately in love with God. Celibates who really are signs of the kingdom are loving and sensitive people, as supportive of others as anyone in the church and in society. What else is the kingdom of God if not an environment of charity?

POPE BENEDICT XVI ON FIDELITY

Speaking to priests at Fatima during a four-day tour of Portugal in May 2010, Pope Benedict XVI said:

"Faithfulness over time is the name of love, a consistent, true and profound love for Christ the Priest.... Fidelity to one's vocation requires courage and trust, but the Lord also wishes that you join forces: that you be concerned for one another and support one another fraternally.... Be especially attentive to those situations where there is a certain weakening of priestly ideals or dedication to activities not fully consonant with what is proper for a minister of Christ. Then is the time to take a firm stand, with an attitude of warm fraternal love, as a brother assisting a brother to 'remain on his feet.'.... With [Mary] and like her, we are free so as to be saints;... free from self so that others may grow in Christ, the true Holy One of the Father and the Shepherd to whom priests, as his presence, lend their voice and their gestures; free to bring to today's world Jesus who died and rose again, Jesus who remains with us until the end of time and who gives himself to all in the most Holy Eucharist.

Immaculate Mother, in this place of grace, called together by the love of your Son Jesus the Eternal High Priest, we sons in the Son and his priests, consecrate ourselves to your maternal heart, in order to carry out faithfully the Father's will...."

> May the Church be thus renewed by priests who are holy, priests transfigured by the grace of him who makes all things new."[2]

CONCLUSION

The center of a priest's life is the altar where he celebrates the mystery of the Holy Eucharist. At the altar the priest offers the sacrifice of Christ's passion and death, but also the Resurrection of the Lord. There is no priest without the Eucharist. There is no Eucharist without the priest. On this theme, Archbishop Fulton Sheen wrote, "*We offer Mass, but do we ever think that we are offered in the Mass?* Our Lord wants no more bullocks or goats; He wants those who 'have crucified nature, with all its passions, all its impulses' (Gal 5:24). St. Augustine said there is no need to look outside oneself for a sheep to offer to God. Each has within him that which he can crucify."[3]

The words of St. Paul should ring in the ears of a priest each time he stands at the altar. "I appeal to you therefore, brothers and sisters, by the mercies of God, to present your bodies as a living sacrifice, holy and acceptable to God, which is your spiritual worship" (Romans 12:1). Christ won our salvation by offering his body to be given up on the cross. Jesus broke bread at the Last Supper but he also was the bread to be broken. Will he recognize priests who fail to be broken bread, who fail to offer their bodies as living sacrifices? Will the priest who fails to be sacrificial fulfill the destiny of his priesthood? Celibacy is a symbol of that dedication. Pouring out oneself for the salvation of parishioners is an effective way of living the eucharistic mystery. There will be no authentic fidelity to priesthood and celibacy without a life that is an extension of the mystery of the cross celebrated each day at the altar.

But there is also an identification with the Resurrection of Christ. The Eucharist is the bread of angels, the bread of life. Over a lifetime, a priest walks time and again away from the altar as one risen with Christ, filled with his love and hope. Moses' face needed to be veiled after encountering God. A priest's face does not need that glow; it is in his heart that the beauty of God appears. This is the ultimate source of the joy of priesthood.

The priest will be involved in every kind of fidelity. He needs to accept the basis of fidelity that claims, "And hope does not disappoint us, because God's love has been poured into our hearts through the Holy Spirit that has been given to us" (Romans 5:5). Like all believers, a priest must be faithful to his true self. He should be the first to live the opening chapter of the catechism on the human capacity for God. A priest's human dignity flows from his longing for God.

I believe a priest may need to post the following dialogue between Jesus and Peter where he can see every day:

> When they had finished breakfast, Jesus said to Simon Peter, "Simon son of John, do you love me more than these?" He said to him, "Yes, Lord; you know that I love you." Jesus said to him, "Feed my lambs." A second time he said to him, "Simon son of John, do you love me?" He said to him, "Yes, Lord; you know that I love you." Jesus said to him, "Tend my sheep." He said to him the third time, "Simon son of John, do you love me?" Peter felt hurt because he said to him the third time, "Do you love me?" And he said to him, "Lord, you know everything; you know that I love you." Jesus said to him, "Feed my sheep." (John 21:15–17)

A priest will be faithful to his friends, if he abides by his commitment to friendship with Christ. It is the secret to feeding God's people. Because of the public nature of parish ministry, a priest will be part of the various ministries in his church, the local communities around him, and the public square in the city, state, and nation. He will be more effective when he is faithful in the responsibilities this entails. A priest is involved in marriage preparation and weddings, as well as sustaining the permanence of marriage and family. His witness and wisdom is a pillar of fidelity for those who struggle to make marriage and family work.

This mosaic of fidelity is a privilege for priests to support, pray for, and sacrifice on behalf of all whom they serve. This can only be done with the help of God, the intercession of Mary and the saints, and a humble awareness of what St. Paul taught that Jesus taught him: "My grace is sufficient for you, for power is made perfect in weakness" (2 Corinthians 12:9).

FOR PERSONAL APPLICATION

1. What qualities have you admired in priests?
2. Why do priests invite parishioners to be active in the parish?
3. Why do you like to see the humanity of the priest?

FOR GROUP DISCUSSION

1. What can you do to strengthen the priest in his calling? If your son wanted to be a priest, how would you react?
2. How can you best support the celibacy of priests?
3. It has been said that the fidelity of priests to their calling encourages the fidelity of married couples to each other and that marital fidelity supports celibate fidelity in priests. What do you think?
4. The idea of married priests comes up now and then. What are the pros and cons?

SCRIPTURE MEDITATION

The Prayer of Jesus

I have made your name known to those whom you gave me from the world. They were yours, and you gave them to me, and they have kept your word. Now they know that everything you have given me is from you; for the words that you gave to me I have given to them, and they have received them and know in truth that I came from you; and they have believed that you sent me.

Sanctify them in the truth; your word is truth. As you have sent me into the world, so I have sent them into the world. And for their sakes I sanctify myself, so that they also may be sanctified in truth.

I ask not only on behalf of these, but also on behalf of those who will believe in me through their word, that they may all be one. As you, Father, are in me and I am in you, may they also be in us, so that the world may believe that you have sent me. (John 17:6–8, 17–21)

PROMISES
I pledge to be faithful to and supportive of our priests by:

_____

_____

_____

_____

_____

_____

_____

_____

_____

INTRODUCTION
1. Timothy Dolan, "Manhattan Declaration: A Call of Christian Conscience," www.manhattandeclaration.org (accessed Oct. 25, 2010).
2. David Brooks, "The Broken Society," www.nytimes.com/2010/03/19/opinion/19brooks.html (accessed Oct. 25, 2010).
3. Ross Douthat, "Let's Talk About Faith," www.nytimes.com/2010/01/11/opinion/11douthat.html (accessed Oct. 25, 2010).
4. Naomi Schaefer Riley, "The Fate of the Spirit," http://online.wsj.com/article/SB10001424052970203440104574399822355625960.html? KEYWORDS=The+Fate+of+the+Spirit (accessed Oct. 25, 2010).

CHAPTER ONE: IF YOU DON'T LOVE, YOU WILL NOT BE FAITHFUL
1. *United States Catholic Catechism for Adults* (Washington, D.C.: United States Conference of Catholic Bishops, 2006), p. 291.
2. Joseph Gomez, *Men of Brave Heart* (Huntington, Ind: Our Sunday Visitor, 2009), p. 196.
3. *The Rites of the Catholic Church*, Vol. II, (New York: Pueblo, 1990), p. 40.
4. Joseph Ratzinger, *Introduction to Christianity* (San Francisco: Ignatius, 1990), p. 252.
5. Alfred McBride, *The Seven Last Words of Jesus* (Cincinnati: St. Anthony Messenger Press, 1990), p. 79.
6. G.K. Chesterton, *Orthodoxy* (Rockville, Md.: Serenity, 2009), p. 29.
7. Chesterton, p. 35.
8. Chesterton, p. 64.

CHAPTER TWO: GOD IS ALWAYS FAITHFUL TO US
1. *The Liturgy of the Hours*, Vol. II, (Totowa, N.J.: Catholic Book, 1976), p. 743.
2. Benedict Groeschel, C.F.R., *Questions and Answers About Your Journey to God,* Huntington, Ind.: Our Sunday Visitor, 2007), p. 96.
3. Austen Ivereigh, "God Makes a Comeback," *America*, October 5, 2009, p. 11.
4. Ivereigh, p. 13.
5. Ivereigh, p. 14.
6. Ivereigh, p. 14.
7. Ivereigh, p. 12.
8. This story about Malcolm Muggeridge was found at http://eSermons.com. For more information about him and his relationship with Mother Teresa, read his book *Something Beautiful for God* (New York: HarperOne, 1986).

CHAPTER THREE: BE FAITHFUL TO YOUR REAL SELF
1. See http://www.vatican.va/archive/catechism/p1s1c1.htm.
2. Charles Pope, "Three Sayings About Marriage," http://blog.adw.org/2010/08/three-sayings-on-marriage (accessed Oct. 25, 2010).

CHAPTER FOUR: STAY FAITHFUL TO YOUR FRIENDS
1. *The Liturgy of the Hours*, Vol. III, p. 400.

CHAPTER FIVE: STAY FAITHFUL TO YOUR COMMUNITIES
1. MacArthur's Farewell available at www.nationalcenter.org/MacArthurFarewell.html (accessed Oct. 25, 2010).
2. Emily Stimpson, "The Power of Pious Practices," *Our Sunday Visitor,* April 4, 2010.
3. Timothy Dolan, "Keeping the Lord's Day Holy," *Gospel in the Digital Age* at http://blog.archny.org/?p=570 (accessed Oct. 25, 2010).

CHAPTER SIX: STAY FAITHFUL TO YOUR MARRIAGE
1. Bradford Wilcox, et al. "Why Marriage Matters: 26 Conclusions from the Social Sciences." See www.americanvalues.org.

CHAPTER SEVEN: BEHOLD, A FAITHFUL PRIEST
1. Adapted from Thomas Kunkel's *Enormous Prayers: A Journey Into Priesthood* (New York: Basic, 1990), pp. 157–165.
2. From "Pope to Consecrated: Fidelity is Greatest Concern," www.zenit.org/article-29231?!=english (accessed Oct. 25, 2010).
3. Fulton Sheen, *The Priest Is Not His Own* (San Francisco: Ignatius, 2005), p. 25.